THE *Indispensable* CALVIN AND HOBBES

A Calvin and Hobbes Treasury by

BILL WATTERSON

Includes cartoons from *The Revenge of the Baby-Sat* and *Scientific Progress Goes "Boink"*

Andrews McMeel
PUBLISHING®

Calvin and Hobbes is distributed internationally
by Andrews McMeel Syndication.

Andrews McMeel Publishing
a division of Andrews McMeel Universal
1130 Walnut Street, Kansas City, Missouri 64106

www.andrewsmcmeel.com

ISBN: 978-1-4494-7235-1

Library of Congress Control Number: 9272248

21 22 23 24 25 SDB 10 9 8 7 6 5 4 3 2

I made a big decision a little while ago.
I don't remember what it was, which prob'ly goes to show
That many times a simple choice can prove to be essential
Even though it often might appear inconsequential.

I must have been distracted when I left my home because
Left or right I'm sure I went. (I wonder which it was!)
Anyway, I never veered: I walked in that direction
Utterly absorbed, it seems, in quiet introspection.

For no reason I can think of, I've wandered far astray.
And that is how I got to where I find myself today.

Explorers are we, intrepid and bold,
Out in the wild, amongst wonders untold.
Equipped with our wits, a map, and a snack,
We're searching for fun and we're on the right track!

My mother has eyes on the back of her head!
I don't quite believe it, but that's what she said.
She explained that she'd been so uniquely endowed
To catch me when I did Things Not Allowed.
I think she must also have eyes on her rear.
I've noticed her hindsight is unusually clear.

At night my mind does not much care
If what it thinks is here or there.
It tells me stories it invents
And makes up things that don't make sense.
I don't know why it does this stuff.
The real world seems quite weird enough.

What if my bones were in a museum,
Where aliens paid good money to see 'em?
And suppose that they'd put me together all wrong,
Sticking bones on to bones where they didn't belong!

Imagine phalanges, pelvis, and spine
Welded to mandibles that once had been mine!
With each misassemblage, the error compounded,
The aliens would draw back in terror, astounded!

Their textbooks would show me in grim illustration,
The most hideous thing ever seen in creation!
The museum would commission a model in plaster
Of ME, to be called, "Evolution's Disaster"!

And paleontologists there would debate
Dozens of theories to help postulate
How man survived for those thousands of years
With teeth-covered arms growing out of his ears!

Oh, I hope that I'm never in such manner displayed,
No matter HOW much to see me the aliens paid.

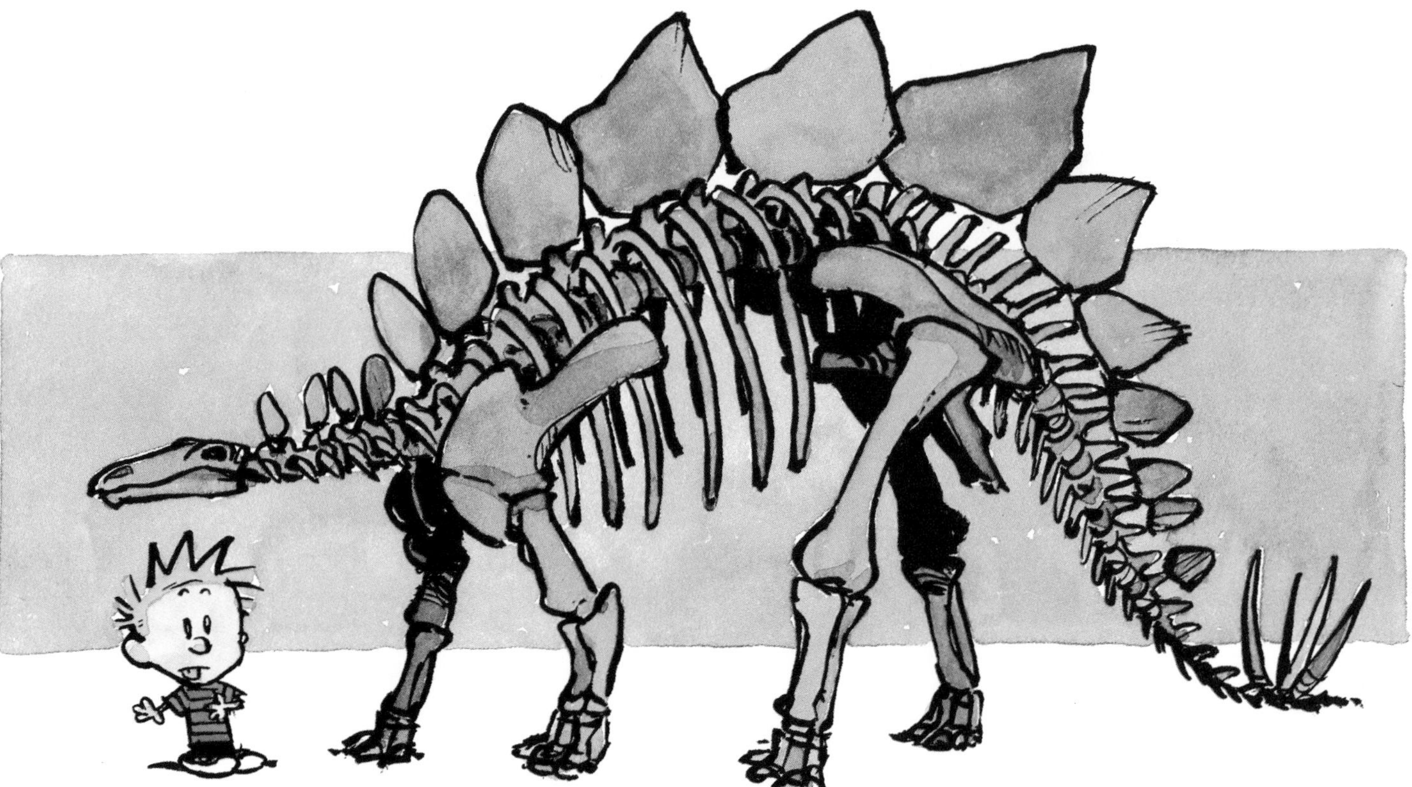

I did not want to go with them.
Alas, I had no choice.
This was made quite clear to me
In threat'ning tones of voice.

I protested mightily
And scrambled 'cross the floor.
But though I grabbed the furniture,
They dragged me out the door.

In the car, I screamed and moaned.
I cried my red eyes dry.
The window down, I yelled for help
To people we passed by.

Mom and Dad can make the rules
And certain things forbid,
But I can make them wish that they
Had never had a kid.

Now I'm in bed,
The sheets pulled to my head.
My tiger is here making Zs.
He's furry and hot.
He takes up a lot
Of the bed and he's hogging the breeze.

WHO MADE THIS MESS OUT HERE ?!

IT WASN'T **ME**, MOM! IT WAS...UH.. IT WAS...
WATTERSON

IT WAS A HORRIBLE LITTLE VENUSIAN WHO MATERIALIZED IN THE KITCHEN! HE TOOK OUT SOME DIABOLICAL HIGH-FREQUENCY DEVICE, POINTED IT AT VARIOUS OBJECTS, AND...

MOTHERS ARE THE NECESSITY OF INVENTION.

I'M HO-OME!

KAPOW

WATTERSON

WHAT DID YOU DO, STEP ON A LAND MINE?
WHEN'S DAD EVER GOING TO BUILD THAT TIGER PIT I KEEP ASKING HIM ABOUT?

CALVIN, WHERE ARE YOU? GET OUT HERE!

COME ON, CALVIN, I'M GETTING TIRED OF THIS!
WATTERSON

I **MEAN** IT, CALVIN! COME OUT AND TAKE YOUR BATH! ***NOW!***

SOONER OR LATER SHE'S GOING TO HAVE TO QUESTION WHETHER THIS IS REALLY WORTH THE TROUBLE.

Calvin and HOBBES

by WATTERSON

THERE'S NO INCOME TO COVER HIS COSTS. HOW DOES HE DO IT?

Calvin and Hobbes
by WATTERSON
HERE WE ARE AT THE TOP OF "DISMEMBERMENT GORGE". READY TO GO DOWN?

HOW ABOUT IF I STEER THIS TIME?
GET ON, YOU BIG SISSY.

I'VE BEEN GOOD ALL DAY SO FAR.

CHRISTMAS IS GETTING NEAR, HUH?
YOU GOT IT.

I'VE BEEN WONDERING, THOUGH. IS IT TRULY BEING GOOD IF THE ONLY REASON I BEHAVE WELL IS SO I CAN GET MORE LOOT AT CHRISTMAS?

I MEAN, REALLY, ALL I'M DOING IS SAYING I CAN BE BRIBED.

IS THAT GOOD ENOUGH, OR DO I HAVE TO BE GOOD IN MY HEART AND SPIRIT?

IN OTHER WORDS, DO I REALLY HAVE TO BE GOOD OR DO I JUST HAVE TO ACT GOOD?
WATTERSON

I SUPPOSE IN YOUR CASE, SANTA WILL HAVE TO TAKE WHAT HE CAN GET.
OK... SO EXACTLY HOW GOOD DO YOU THINK I HAVE TO ACT? REALLY GOOD, OR JUST PRETTY GOOD?

WANT TO READ MY LETTER TO SANTA ?
ALL THAT ?!

I HOPE I DIDN'T FORGET TO ASK FOR SOMETHING I WANT.
THIS IS ALPHABETIZED.

YEAH, AND I CROSS-INDEXED THE ACCESSORY ITEMS HE'LL NEED TO GET. I TRY TO HELP HIM OUT.
THIS SAYS, "VOLUME ONE."

"ATOM BOMB" THROUGH "GRENADE LAUNCHER."
YOU'RE GOING TO BE ONE SAD LITTLE KID ON CHRISTMAS MORNING.

IT SNOWED LAST NIGHT! TURN ON THE RADIO! MAYBE THEY CLOSED SCHOOL!

MAYBE THE SCHOOL BUSES ALL FROZE UP! MAYBE THE PRINCIPAL CAN'T GET OUT OF HIS DRIVEWAY!

GET DRESSED, CALVIN. IT ONLY SNOWED AN INCH.

GETTING AN INCH OF SNOW IS LIKE WINNING 10 CENTS IN THE LOTTERY.

A LONE KNIGHT CHARGES UP THE HILL TOWARD THE GIANT CAVE AT THE TOP.

IMMEDIATELY THE MONSTROUS DRAGON LUNGES OUT AND SPEWS A RAGING FIREBALL!

THE KNIGHT IS FRIED TO A CRUNCHY CRISP... HIS ARMOR FUSED INTO A SOLID PIECE! THE DRAGON CIRCLES OVERHEAD, DARING OTHER FOOLS TO COME AFTER HIM!

DID YOU BRUSH YOUR TEETH?
COME HERE AND SEE!

I'm gonna pound you in gym class, shrimp.

GET YOUR KICKS **NOW**, YOU GLANDULAR FREAK, BECAUSE ONCE YOU GROW UP YOU CAN'T GO BEATING PEOPLE UP FOR NO REASON!

Yeah, I guess you're right.

THAT REALLY WASN'T WHAT I MEANT AT ALL.

WHAT GRADE DID YOU GET?
I GOT AN "A".

REALLY? BOY, I'D HATE TO BE YOU. I GOT A "C."

WHY ON EARTH WOULD YOU RATHER GET A "C" THAN AN "A"?!

I FIND MY LIFE IS A LOT EASIER THE LOWER I KEEP EVERYONE'S EXPECTATIONS.

WHY DO I HAVE TO WEAR THESE DORKY CLOTHES AND GET MY HAIR COMBED?!

YOUR DAD'S GOING TO TAKE YOUR PICTURE. HOLD STILL.
I DON'T ***WANT*** TO GET MY PICTURE TAKEN!
IT WILL JUST TAKE A FEW MINUTES. WE'RE GOING TO PUT THE PICTURE OF YOU IN OUR CHRISTMAS CARDS SO EVERYONE CAN SEE WHAT YOU LOOK LIKE NOW.

WHAT A DUMB IDEA. WHY ARE WE DOING ***THAT***?
SO WE WON'T HAVE RELATIVES DROPPING BY TO VISIT.
DEAR...

I DON'T HAVE MUCH FILM LEFT, SO STOP MAKING FACES WHEN I TAKE THE PICTURE, OR YOUR NAME'S MUD.

Calvin and Hobbes

by WATTERSON

DO YOU THINK MONSTERS ARE UNDER THE BED TONIGHT?

I DON'T KNOW. HOW CAN YOU TELL WITHOUT LOOKING?

ONE WAY IS TO TELL A STORY ABOUT A LITTLE KID GETTING MAULED AND EATEN ALIVE.
HOW DOES *THAT* TELL YOU IF YOU HAVE MONSTERS?
SOMETIMES THEY LAUGH.

I'M FREEZING! WHY DO WE KEEP THIS HOUSE SO DARN COLD?!

CRANK UP THE THERMOSTAT AND BUILD A FIRE, WILL YA?
I HAVE A BETTER IDEA. C'MERE.

OK, STEP OUTSIDE.
WHY? WHAT'S OUTSIDE?

IN A FEW MINUTES YOU CAN COME IN, AND THEN THE HOUSE WILL SEEM NICE AND WARM.
I'M TELLING THE NEWSPAPERS ABOUT YOU, DAD!

READ ME "HAMSTER HUEY AND THE GOOEY KABLOOIE."
OH, I DON'T WANT TO READ THAT AGAIN. LET'S READ SOMETHING DIFFERENT TONIGHT.

NO, I WANT TO HEAR "HAMSTER HUEY AND THE GOOEY KABLOOIE."
C'MON, CALVIN, I'VE READ THIS A THOUSAND TIMES.

READ IT AGAIN. PLEASE? ***PLEASE***?
ALL RIGHT, ALL RIGHT.

YOU'LL DO THE SQUEAKY VOICES, THE GOOSHY SOUND EFFECTS, AND THE HAPPY HAMSTER HOP, WON'T YOU?
LOOK, CAN'T WE READ SOMETHING ELSE?

MOMM! MOM!

WHAT IS IT? WHAT'S THE MATTER?
DO PEOPLE GROW FROM SPORES?

SPORES?!? YOU WAKE ME UP AT 2 AM TO ASK IF PEOPLE GROW FROM SPORES? ARE YOU OUT OF YOUR MIND?? WHY ARE YOU EVEN AWAKE?! GO TO SLEEP!!

SHE DIDN'T ANSWER. SHE MUST NOT KNOW.
I'M TELLING YOU, IT'S TRUE.
WATTERSON

I SAY IT'S A FALLACY THAT KIDS NEED 12 YEARS OF SCHOOL! THREE MONTHS IS PLENTY!

LOOK AT ME. I'M SMART! I DON'T NEED 11½ MORE YEARS OF SCHOOL! IT'S A COMPLETE WASTE OF MY TIME!

HOW ON EARTH DID YOU GET ALL THE WAY TO THE BUS STOP WITH BOTH FEET THROUGH ONE PANT LEG?
I FELL DOWN A LOT.

...WHY? WHAT'S YOUR POINT?
NOTHING. I WAS JUST CURIOUS.
WATTERSON

HOW'S MY PEANUT BUTTER SANDWICH COMING? YOU'RE USING CHUNKY PEANUT BUTTER, RIGHT? I WON'T EAT SMOOTH!

MAKE IT AN OPEN FACE SANDWICH, TOO! DON'T PUT ANY JELLY ON IT OR ANYTHING! AND USE SOME NORMAL BREAD! I DON'T LIKE THOSE WEIRD GRAIN BREADS!

DID YOU CUT IT DIAGONALLY? I LIKE TRIANGLES BETTER THAN RECTANGLES, SO BE SURE TO CUT IT RIGHT!

YOUR MAJESTY'S SANDWICH.
HEY, THIS IS A CLOSED-FACE, HORIZONTALLY CUT, SMOOTH PEANUT BUTTER SANDWICH ON WEIRD BREAD WITH JELLY! WEREN'T YOU LISTENING?!
WATTERSON

Calvin and HOBBES
by WATTERSON
THAT'S NICE.
I'M LEAVING OUT A SANDWICH FOR SANTA.

WHAT DO YOU THINK HE'D LIKE WITH THAT? SOME MILK?
I THINK "SANTA" WOULD RATHER HAVE A COLD BEER.
DEAR!

PSST! WAKE UP! IT'S CHRISTMAS!
ARE YOU SURE? IT'S STILL DARK OUT.

IT'S FOUR IN THE MORNING! LET'S SEE IF SANTA LEFT OUR LOOT YET!
OH BOY!

WE'LL LET MOM AND DAD SLEEP ANOTHER HOUR, BUT WE CAN AT LEAST COUNT ALL OUR PACKAGES.
I GET TO PLUG IN THE TREE LIGHTS!

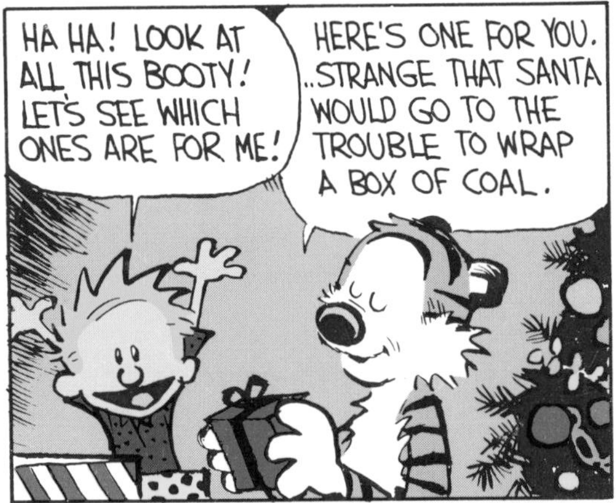
HA HA! LOOK AT ALL THIS BOOTY! LET'S SEE WHICH ONES ARE FOR ME!
HERE'S ONE FOR YOU. ..STRANGE THAT SANTA WOULD GO TO THE TROUBLE TO WRAP A BOX OF COAL.

HAR HAR. HERE'S ONE FOR MOM... HERE'S ONE FOR ME... THIS ONE IS FOR DAD... HEY, WHERE ARE YOUR PRESENTS? SANTA GOOFED UP!
GOOD THING WE TIGERS ARE NATURALLY GIFTED TO BEGIN WITH.

MOMM! DAAAD! SANTA DIDN'T BRING HOBBES ANYTHING!
UH OH. THINK QUICK, DEAR.
IT HAD BETTER BE A LOT LATER THAN IT FEELS LIKE.
WATTERSON

WELL, HERE'S A PRESENT FROM ME ANYWAY. HOPE IT FITS.
THE BEST PRESENTS DON'T COME IN BOXES. I'LL TREASURE THIS ONE FOREVER.

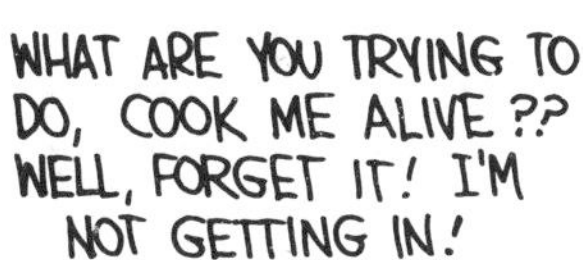

NOTHING EVER CHANGES. IT'S JUST SCHOOL, SCHOOL, SCHOOL.

BOY, DID I GET IN TROUBLE AT SCHOOL TODAY. WOW.
WHAT HAPPENED?

I DON'T EVEN WANT TO TALK ABOUT IT.

DID IT HAVE ANYTHING TO DO WITH ALL THOSE SIRENS ABOUT NOON?
I SAID I DON'T WANT TO TALK ABOUT IT.
WATTERSON

DID YOU BRING SOMETHING FOR SHOW AND TELL?
YOU BET!

I BROUGHT THESE CHARRED ROCKS AND ASHES FROM MY BACK YARD.
WATTERSON

SEE? DRAMATIC PROOF THAT UFOs LANDED NOT A HUNDRED FEET FROM MY HOUSE! THEIR RETRO ROCKETS BURNED SOLID ROCK INTO THIS FRAGILE GRAY DUST CUBE!

THIS IS AN OLD CHARCOAL BRIQUETTE.
EVEN AS WE SPEAK, ALIENS ARE UNDOUBTEDLY INFILTRATING THE HIGHEST LEVELS OF OUR GOVERNMENT.

DISGUSTING DENIZEN OF THE DEEP, THE GIANT OCTOPUS GLIDES ACROSS THE OCEAN FLOOR.

AT THE SIGHT OF AN ENEMY, HE RELEASES A CLOUD OF INK AND MAKES HIS GETAWAY!
WATTERSON

MISS WORMWOOD!

Calvin and Hobbes
by WATTERSON
WELL, IT'S A NEW YEAR.

AND I'D SAY THE FIRST 10 HOURS HAVEN'T BEEN UP TO SNUFF.

DID YOU MAKE ANY NEW YEAR'S RESOLUTIONS ?

YOU BET! I RESOLVED TO QUIT HIDING MY FEELINGS SO MUCH! FROM NOW ON, THE WORLD'S GONNA KNOW EXACTLY WHAT I THINK OF IT!

YES, YOU'VE CERTAINLY BEEN THE MODEL OF SELF-RESTRAINT AND UNDER-STATEMENT UP UNTIL NOW.
WELL NO MORE.

AND I'VE ALSO RESOLVED NOT TO PUT UP WITH SARCASTIC TIGERS.
IF I SEE ANY, I'LL TELL THEM.
WATTERSON

SHOVEL, SHOVEL, SHOVEL!

WHY CAN'T WE GET A SNOW BLOWER?? WE MUST BE THE ONLY FAMILY IN THE WORLD THAT STILL SHOVELS THE DRIVEWAY BY HAND! I'M FREEZING!

IT BUILDS CHARACTER. KEEP AT IT.

PRETTY CONVENIENT HOW EVERY TIME ***I*** BUILD CHARACTER, ***HE*** SAVES A COUPLE HUNDRED DOLLARS.

NEXT TIME WE GO DOWN, ***I*** GET TO STEER THE SLED.

YOU?! YOU STEER LIKE AN OLD LADY!
YEAH, WELL, I'M SICK OF GOING OVER AND THROUGH EVERY OBSTACLE ON THE HILL.

"EVERY OBSTACLE"?!? WE MISSED THE BRIAR PATCH, DIDN'T WE?!

BY GOING DOWN THE GULLY AND INTO THE STREAM, YES.
OH, YOU MAKE EVERYTHING SOUND SO TERRIBLE. YOU SHOULD BE GLAD WE'RE ALIVE.

THIS IS THE FINEST SNOWBALL EVER MADE!

PAINSTAKINGLY HAND-CRAFTED INTO A PERFECT SPHERE FROM A SECRET MIXTURE OF SLUSH, ICE, DIRT, DEBRIS AND FINE POWDER SNOW, THIS ***IS*** THE ULTIMATE WINTER WEAPON!

YES, THIS MARVEL OF CRYSTALLINE ENGINEERING WI..
WHAP!!

ANOTHER CASUALTY OF THE SEDUCTION OF ART.

WHAT DO YOU THINK IS THE BEST WAY TO GET WHAT YOU WANT? IS IT BETTER TO HOLD FAST AND NEVER BACK DOWN, OR TO COMPROMISE?

I SUPPOSE IT'S BEST TO HOLD FAST WHEN YOU CAN, AND COMPROMISE WHEN YOU NEED TO.

THAT'S A LOT MORE MATURE THAN I THINK I CARE TO BE.

I THINK THE SHORT ATTENTION SPAN OF TELEVISION IS GREAT.

AS FAR AS *I'M* CONCERNED, IF SOMETHING IS SO COMPLICATED THAT YOU CAN'T EXPLAIN IT IN 10 SECONDS, THEN IT'S PROBABLY NOT WORTH KNOWING ANYWAY.

MY TIME IS VALUABLE. I CAN'T GO THINKING ABOUT ONE SUBJECT FOR MINUTES ON END. I'M A BUSY MAN.

...WHO'S BEEN SITTING HERE FOR THREE HOURS.
... AT SIX THOUGHTS A MINUTE.

THERE'S SOMETHING MAGICAL ABOUT HAVING A FIRE.

THE CRACKLES AND SNAPS, THE WARM, FLICKERING LIGHT... EVERYTHING ALWAYS SEEMS SAFE AND COZY IF YOU'RE SITTING IN FRONT OF A FIRE.

AND IF YOU'VE GOT A HOT TIGER TUMMY TO LIE AGAINST.... **WELL!**
Z

Calvin and HOBBES
by WATTERSON
C'MON, WE'D BETTER GO OUTSIDE FOR A WHILE.
HOW COME?

MOM'S GETTING THAT LOOK.

THIS WILL BE THE BEST SNOW FORT EVER BUILT!

OK, THE MAIN FORTRESS WILL BE A WALL FIVE FEET HIGH, AND GO FROM HERE DOWN OVER THAT HILL, WITH TURRETS EVERY 50 FEET.

OVER HERE WE'LL BUILD AN INNER WALL, IN CASE WE HAVE TO RETREAT, AND A BIN TO HOLD OUR SNOW BALL RESERVES.
GOT IT.

HMM... THE SNOW DOESN'T PACK TOO WELL, DOES IT?
IT'S NOT WET ENOUGH.

GOSH, IT'LL TAKE FOREVER JUST TO BUILD THE OUTER WALL... EVEN WITHOUT THE TURRETS.
I'M COLD.

ME, TOO. LET'S GO IN.
MAYBE WE CAN HAVE SOME HOT CHOCOLATE BY A FIRE!

THIS IS MORE FUN THAN ACTUALLY BUILDING THE FORT ANYWAY. NOW WHERE SHOULD WE PUT THE ICICLE SPIKES?
ALL ALONG THE OUTER WALL, AFTER THE MOAT. ...SAY, I THINK YOU GOT MORE MARSHMALLOWS IN YOUR HOT CHOCOLATE THAN I DID.
SNOW FORT
WATTERSON

THE BAY DOORS OPEN AND OUT FALLS CALVIN, THE C-BOMB!

CALVIN IS ABOUT TO UNLEASH THE PURE DESTRUCTIVE FORCE OF A MILLION A-BOMBS!

THE WORLD GASPS IN HORROR AS HE STREAKS TOWARD HIS TARGET!

OH NO YOU DON'T!!

WILL YOU READ THIS TONIGHT?
"AN ODE TO TIGERS"?

HOBBES WROTE IT.
"THE ZEBRA'S STRIPES ARE LACKING HUES, SO THEY DON'T COMPARE TO YOU-KNOW-WHOSE."
"ORANGE, BLACK AND WHITE IS WHAT TO WEAR! IT'S HAUTE COUTURE FOR THOSE WHO DARE! IT'S CAMOUFLAGE, AND STYLISH, TOO! YES, TIGERS LOOK THE BEST, IT'S TRUE!"

THIS GOES ON?
FOR PAGES. PRETTY TEDIOUS, ISN'T IT?

I'M HO-OME!

KAPOW!
WUMPH!

GREAT. THE SNOW CUSHIONED THE BLOW TO MY SPINE, SO NOW I CAN DIE OF PNEUMONIA.
AWW, HAS OO GOT DE SNIFFOOS?

Calvin and Hobbes
by WATTERSON
PUT 'ER DOWN HERE.

YOU KNOW, THESE THINGS SHOULD REALLY COME WITH AIR BAGS.

READY?
READY.

OFF WE GO-O!

OOH!

YIKES!

WOW!

SEE? I TOLD YOU.
HELP ME GATHER UP THE SLED, YOU SISSY.
WATTERSON

I LIKE THESE COLD, GRAY WINTER DAYS.

DAYS LIKE THESE LET YOU SAVOR A BAD MOOD.
WATTERSON

YOU TRY IT AND I'LL WATCH.
SISSY.
WATTERSON

LOOK, I PUT A SNOWBALL ON TOP OF THIS SNOWMAN'S HEAD.

NOW I'LL BE THE NEXT WILLIAM TELL, AND I'LL HIT THE SNOWBALL CLEAN OFF!

WATTERSON

OUCH.
AHHH! HE FLINCHED!

Calvin and HOBBES
by WATTERSON

OK, LET'S SEE... IF THE WIND IS BLOWING NORTH-NORTHEAST AT 6 MPH, AND I THROW THE SNOWBALL DUE WEST AT 90 MPH WITH A SLIGHT TOP SPIN....

HA! SUSIE DIDN'T EVEN HEAR ME SNEAK UP!

NOW I'LL CREAM HER CRANIUM WITH A BARRAGE OF SNOWBALLS!

WHIZZZ
PIFF
PIFF

THESE DARN CROSS BREEZES! SHE DIDN'T EVEN NOTICE!

YOU'RE THE WORST SHOT IN THE WORLD, CALVIN! IF IT WASN'T FOR GRAVITY, YOU PROBABLY COULDN'T EVEN HIT THE GROUND!

SMACK!

I DID IT! I DID IT! JUST WHEN IT REALLY COUNTED, I DID IT! HA HA HA! RIGHT IN THE KISSER! HA HA!

BAD NEWS, MOM. I PROMISED MY SOUL TO THE DEVIL THIS AFTERNOON.
OH? THAT RECENTLY?
WATTERSON

THE FEARLESS SPACEMAN SPIFF FINDS HIMSELF ON THE PLANET CLOSEST TO STAR X-351!

AN ALIEN APPROACHES... BUT IN THE BLINDING LIGHT, OUR HERO CAN HARDLY MAKE IT OUT! IS IT FRIENDLY OR HOSTILE?

WHAT ARE YOU DOING IN BED STILL?! GET READY FOR SCHOOL!

DEFINITELY HOSTILE.

THE SCHOOL BUS WILL BE HERE ANY MINUTE! GO! SCOOT!

SPACEMAN SPIFF, CAPTURED BY VICIOUS ZOGWARGS, IS ABOUT TO BE TRANSPORTED TO THE LABOR CAMP! OUR HERO HATCHES A BOLD PLAN!

AT THE LAST SECOND, SPIFF MAKES HIS BREAK! TAKING ADVANTAGE OF THE PLANET'S WEAKER GRAVITY, OUR HERO IS AWAY LIKE A SHOT.

THERE'S THE BUS... BUT WHY DON'T I SEE CALVIN?

SPIFF ESCAPES!

DID CALVIN GET ON THE BUS?
I DIDN'T SEE. ...WHY?

SOMEONE JUST DARTED BEHIND THAT TREE. SEE, THERE HE GOES AGAIN! ISN'T THAT CALVIN?

THE ZOGWARGS HAVE SPOTTED HIM! OUR HERO INFLATES THE EMERGENCY JET PACK HE KEEPS IN HIS POCKET, AND PREPARES FOR TAKEOFF!

CALVIN, WHAT ARE YOU DOING? YOU'RE SUPPOSED TO BE ON THE SCHOOL BUS! GET OVER HERE!

OUR HERO BLASTS OFF WITH HIS EMERGENCY JET PACK! ANOTHER DARING ESCAPE FOR THE INTREPID SPACEMAN SPIFF!

ZOUNDS! THE ZOGWARGS ARE ON ROCKET SCOOTERS! SPIFF FIRES HIS DEATH RAY BLASTER!

IT'S YOUR OWN GRAVE YOU'RE DIGGING, BUSTER!
WATERSON

YOUNG MAN, YOU ARE IN VERY BIG TROUBLE!

WHY DIDN'T YOU GET ON THE SCHOOL BUS?! NOW I'VE GOT TO DRIVE YOU, AND YOUR DAD WILL BE LATE FOR WORK!

YOU'VE INCONVENIENCED EVERYONE! WHAT HAVE YOU GOT TO SAY FOR YOURSELF?!

GIVE ME LIBERTY OR GIVE ME DEATH, ZOGWARG QUEEN!
DON'T TEMPT ME! AND LISTEN, YOU CALL ME "MOM," ...GOT IT?
WATERSON

HEY, CALVIN, HOW COME YOU'RE LATE TODAY? WHY DIDN'T YOU RIDE THE BUS?

I WAS GOING TO SKIP SCHOOL, BUT I GOT CAUGHT.
REALLY? HOW?

MOM HAD THE WIND FOR THAT FINAL SPRINT.

YOUR MOM HAD TO CHASE YOU?
I COULDN'T BELIEVE IT WHEN SHE CLEARED THE HEDGE.
WATERSON

YES, CAN I HAVE THE TOOL DEPARTMENT, PLEASE? THANK YOU.

HELLO? HOW MUCH ARE YOUR POWER CIRCULAR SAWS? I SEE. AND YOUR ELECTRIC DRILLS? UH-HUH. HOW BIG OF A BIT WILL THAT HOLD? REALLY? GREAT.

SO THE ASSIGNMENT IS PAGES TWO THROUGH FOUR? OK, THANKS SUSIE.

..SORRY ABOUT THAT. DO YOU CARRY ACETYLENE TORCHES? OK, RING IT ALL UP. THIS WILL BE ON MASTERCARD.

LOOK AT ALL THIS HOMEWORK I'M SUPPOSED TO DO!

I DON'T WANT TO DO THIS GARBAGE! I WANT TO GO PLAY OUTSIDE!

CHILDHOOD IS SHORT AND MATURITY IS FOREVER.

PEOPLE ARE ROTTEN.

WHEN I GROW UP, I'M GOING TO LIVE A MILLION MILES AWAY FROM EVERYONE!

HOW WILL YOU SURVIVE? WHAT WILL YOU EAT?

...WELL, MOM COULD COME BY TWICE A DAY TO COOK, I SUPPOSE.
THAT WOULD BE QUITE A COMMUTE.

GET A LOAD OF THIS DUMB ASSIGNMENT! I'M SUPPOSED TO WRITE ABOUT AN ADVENTURE I'VE HAD!

I HAVEN'T HAD ANY ADVENTURES! MY LIFE HAS BEEN ONE BIG BORE FROM THE BEGINNING!
WATTERSON

HAVE I EVER BEEN ABDUCTED BY PIRATES? HAVE I EVER FACED DOWN A CHARGING RHINO? HAVE I EVER BEEN IN A SHOOT-OUT, OR ON A BOMBING RAID? NO! I NEVER GET TO HAVE ADVENTURES!

WHAT ABOUT THE TIME YOU BACKED THE CAR THROUGH THE GARAGE DOOR?
YOU CALL THAT AN ADVENTURE? I DIDN'T EVEN GET ON THE HIGHWAY.

WHEN DO YOU THINK WE'LL GET A THUNDER AND LIGHTNING STORM?

I DON'T KNOW. PROBABLY NOT UNTIL SPRING.

I THINK HE'S GOING TO MELT BEFORE WE CAN BRING HIM TO LIFE.
WATTERSON

HEY, SUSIE, STAND ON THIS "X."
WHY?

NO REASON. JUST DO IT. I DARE YOU.
NO.

PLEASE? C'MON!
GET LOST.

THIS MAY NOT WORK OUT AS WELL AS I THOUGHT.
WATTERSON

Calvin and HOBBES
by WATTERSON
THE VALIANT SPACEMAN SPIFF IS LED BY HIS CAPTORS TO A SECRET DUNGEON TO BE DEBRIEFED!

LITTLE DO THEY REALIZE THAT OUR HERO DOESN'T WEAR BRIEFS!

EAT YOUR DINNER, CALVIN.
UGH.

POISED PRECARIOUSLY OVER A PERCOLATING PIT OF PUTRID PASTA, SPACEMAN SPIFF IS HELD PRISONER!
STILL WONT TALK, EH, EARTHLING?

OUR HERO'S MIND RACES FURIOUSLY!
HE'S HAD HIS CHANCE! LET'S MAKE HIM EAT!

LOOK BEHIND YOU!!

KAPWINNGG!

FOOL! THE HUMAN SCUM ESCAPED!
NOT FOR LONG, ZOKBAR-2! AND TOMORROW MORNING HE'LL HAVE COLD MANICOTTI FOR BREAKFAST!
WATTERSON

WOW, YOU'VE MADE A LOT OF SNOWMEN TODAY!

YEP. THEY'RE EFFIGIES. EACH ONE REPRESENTS SOMEONE I HATE.

WHEN THE SUN COMES OUT, I'LL WATCH THEIR FEATURES SLOWLY MELT DOWN THEIR DRIPPING BODIES UNTIL THEY'RE NOTHING BUT NOSES AND EYES FLOATING IN POOLS OF WATER.

I WASN'T AWARE YOU EVEN KNEW THIS MANY PEOPLE.
THE ONES I **REALLY** HATE ARE SMALL, SO THEY'LL GO FASTER.

I'M WRITING A BOOK ABOUT MY LIFE.

IT'S CALLED, "CALVIN: THE SHOCKING TRUE STORY OF THE BOY WHOSE EXPLOITS PANICKED A NATION."

INTERESTING TITLE.
THANKS.

SPECIFICALLY WHAT EXPLOITS ARE YOU REFERRING TO?
THAT'S THE PROBLEM. CAN YOU HELP ME THINK OF SOME I COULD DO?

HI, SUSIE.
GO AWAY, CALVIN! SIT SOMEWHERE ELSE! I DON'T WANT TO KNOW WHAT REVOLTING THING YOU HAVE FOR LUNCH TODAY.

RELAX, SUSIE. I'M NOT GOING TO TELL YOU WHAT I HAVE.
YOU'D BETTER NOT. I MEAN IT.

ALL I'LL SAY IS THAT I SURE FEEL SORRY FOR MY TAPEWORM.

MISS WORMWOOD!
HEY! DID I **SAY** WHAT MY LUNCH IS?! **DID** I ?!?

Calvin and HOBBES

by WATTERSON

WHAT'S THIS?
A CRASH TEST DUMMY. NOW I CAN SEE IF THE HILL IS SAFE TO GO DOWN.

OFF YOU GO!

OOH, I THINK I'M GOING TO BE SICK.
WELL I WOULDN'T HAVE STEERED LIKE *THAT!* HE DESERVED IT!

OH, NO! THE AIR PRESSURE IN THIS ROOM IS TOO HIGH!

CALVIN'S ORGANS ARE IN DANGER OF COLLAPSING! HE...HE'S ABOUT TO IMPLODE!

WE'VE GOT TO GET OUT OF HERE! THERE'S TOO MUCH ATMOSPHERE!
SIT STILL AND BEHAVE. WE CAN'T EAT AT FAST FOOD PLACES ALL THE TIME.

THESE TELEVISION PROGRAMS SURE ARE ROTTEN.

THERE ISN'T AN OUNCE OF IMAGINATION IN THE WHOLE BUNCH. WHAT BILGE.

WHO DO THEY THINK IS STUPID ENOUGH TO SIT AND WATCH THIS TRASH?

YOU.
IF THERE WAS ANYTHING **BETTER** ON, I'D WATCH ***THAT.***

Calvin and Hobbes
by WATTERSON
MPH! GET YOUR HAND OUT OF MY EYE!
HOLD STILL. NOW BOOST! LIFT! C'MON!

OK, FORWARD!
ON THE WAY BACK, YOU'RE CARRYING ME.

HEY, I GOT SOME MAIL!

IT'S A VALENTINE CARD.
FROM SUSIE DERKINS!

IT SAYS, "PLEASE BE MY VALEN-TINE."
YOU'RE SUSIE'S VALENTINE!

I'M NOT HER VALENTINE JUST BECAUSE I GOT THIS IN THE MAIL, AM I? DOES THE POST-MASTER GENERAL KNOW ABOUT THIS?
CALVIN AND SUSIE, SITTING IN A TREE-EE! KAY-EYE-ESS-ESS EYE-EN-GEE!

I DON'T HAVE TO KISS HER, DO I ?! IS THAT WHAT VALENTINES DO ??! OH, GROSS!
FIRST COMES LO-OVE, THEN COMES MARRIAGE THEN COMES A BABY IN A BABY CARRIAGE!

THIS CAN'T BE HAPPENING! I NEED A LAWYER! SHE CAN'T MAKE ME BE HER VALENTINE!
HERE SHE COMES! HERE COMES SUSIE!

HI, CALVIN.
GET AWAY FROM ME! I'M NOT YOUR VALEN-TINE! TAKE YOUR CARD BACK! EWW! GIRLS! YECCHH!
WATTERSON

THAT CARD WASN'T FOR YOU, YOU MORON. DIDN'T YOU READ THE BACK OF THE ENVELOPE?
THE BACK?

"CALVIN, PLEASE GIVE THIS TO HOBBES."
HOBBES?!
ME? REALLY? HOT DOG! SMOOCH CITY, HERE I COME!

YOU'RE TAKING A SHOWER NOW? THAT MEANS YOU'RE GOING OUT TONIGHT, RIGHT?
WATTERSON

AND YOU HAVEN'T TOLD ME TO GET CLEANED UP, SO THAT MEANS I'M STAYING HOME, RIGHT?

AND IF I'M STAYING HOME, THAT MEANS YOU'VE GOTTEN ME A BABY SITTER, RIGHT? AND THAT MEANS YOU'VE PROBABLY HIRED ROSALYN, RIGHT?!?

BRILLIANT, HOLMES.
AAAHH HHHHH!

QUICK, HOBBES! WE'VE GOT TO HIDE! MOM AND DAD GOT ROSALYN FOR OUR BABY SITTER AGAIN! AND YOU KNOW WHAT THAT MEANS!

IT USUALLY MEANS WE'RE IN BED BY 6:30.
RIGHT! NO TV, NO HORSING AROUND, NOTHING! SHE JUST WALKS IN AND SENDS US STRAIGHT TO BED!

AND THEN SHE DOESN'T EVEN KISS US GOOD NIGHT.
EWW, GROSS! YOU WANT HER TO?!?
WATTERSON

WHERE ARE YOU GOING TONIGHT? WHY CAN'T HOBBES AND I COME? WHY DO WE HAVE TO HAVE A BABY SITTER?

WE'RE GOING TO DINNER AND A MOVIE JUST TO HAVE SOME TIME TO OURSELVES, OK?

BUT WE COULD COME! HOBBES PROMISES NOT TO KILL ANYONE! WE'D BE GOOD! REALLY! WHY WON'T YOU LET US COME? WHY DON'T YOU WANT US AROUND?

IS THE MOVIE DIRTY? WHAT'S THE PROBLEM?!
GOSH, A DINNER WITH REAL PAUSES IN THE CONVERSATION! CAN YOU IMAGINE?
WATTERSON

HI, ROSALYN. COME ON IN. CALVIN'S UPSTAIRS HIDING FROM YOU, SO YOU MAY HAVE AN EASY EVENING.

THAT WOULD BE GREAT. I'VE GOT TO STUDY TONIGHT FOR A BIG TEST TOMORROW.

DID YOU HEAR THAT? DID YOU HEAR THAT?
HEE HEE!

TONIGHT: THE REVENGE OF THE BABY-SAT!

HI, ROSALYN! HOW ARE YOU? WHAT ARE YOU DOING? HOME-WORK?

RIGHT. I'VE GOT TO STUDY FOR AN EXAM TOMORROW, SO I WANT IT QUIET TONIGHT. GOT IT?

OH, YOU BET, ROZ. HOBBES AND I WON'T MAKE A PEEP. CAN I SEE WHAT YOU'RE STUDYING?
DON'T TOUCH ANYTH...

I GOT HER NOTES! I GOT HER NOTES! RUN, HOBBES, RUN!!
CAL-VIN!

GIVE ME BACK MY NOTES, YOU LITTLE CREEP!
RUN! RUN!

WHAT ARE WE GOING TO DO? SHE'LL KILL US!
INTO THE BATHROOM!

LOCK THE DOOR! QUICK!
CALVIN!
CLICK

OPEN THIS DOOR, OR YOUR PARENTS WILL NEVER FIND YOUR REMAINS!
BOY, SOME BABY SITTER!
HERE GO YOUR NOTES!

CALVIN, YOU'VE GOT TWO SECONDS TO UNLOCK THIS DOOR AND GIVE ME BACK MY SCIENCE NOTES!

YOU KNOW, ROSALYN, I'D SUGGEST YOU ADOPT A MORE HUMBLE ATTITUDE. YOU WOULDN'T WANT ANYTHING TO HAPPEN TO THESE NOTES, WOULD YOU?

YOU SCUMMY LITTLE TROLL! WHEN YOUR PARENTS GET HOME, I'LL...

FLUSH
AUGH!
THERE'S ONE PAGE!

YOU'D BETTER NOT HAVE REALLY FLUSHED ANY OF MY NOTES! I'VE GOT A BIG TEST TOMORROW!

WELL THEN, WITH THAT AT STAKE, OUR DEMANDS SHOULD SEEM VERY REASONABLE!

DEMANDS?! YOU DON'T GET ANY DEMANDS! UNLOCK THIS DOOR!

BOY, YOU'D THINK A HIGH SCHOOL SENIOR WOULD CATCH ON QUICKER. WE SHOULD WRITE THE SCHOOL BOARD.
TORPEDO TUBE READY, CAP'N!

I SURE HOPE YOU MEMORIZED THIS PAGE ALREADY, BECAUSE YOU'RE NEVER GOING TO SEE IT AGAIN!

NO! DON'T FLUSH IT! TELL ME WHAT YOUR STUPID DEMANDS ARE.

THAT'S MORE LIKE IT! OK, FIRST WE WANT TO STAY UP UNTIL MY PARENTS DRIVE IN. SECOND, WE WANT YOU TO GO PICK UP A PIZZA AND RENT US A VIDEO PLAYER...

YOU'RE OUT OF YOUR MIND!
THIRD ... ARE YOU WRITING THESE DOWN?

I DON'T HEAR HER OUT THERE ANYMORE.
ROSALYN?? ARE YOU LISTENING? WE HAVE MORE DEMANDS!

DO YOU THINK SHE WENT AWAY?
WHY WOULD SHE? WE'VE STILL GOT HER SCIENCE NOTES.

DOESN'T SHE WANT THEM ANYMORE? WHAT'S SHE DOING?
MAYBE SHE'S CALLING THE FIRE DEPARTMENT TO AX OPEN THE DOOR.

REALLY? YOU THINK SO? GOSH, THAT'D BE GREAT! REAL FIREMEN WITH REAL AXES! I HOPE THEY DRIVE THEIR BIGGEST FIRE TRUCK!
I HOPE YOUR PARENTS ARE HAVING A RESTFUL EVENING.
WATTERSON

ROSALYN? ARE YOU OUT HERE? ARE YOU CALLING THE FIRE DEPARTME...

GOTCHA!
OH NO!

I DIDN'T REALLY FLUSH YOUR NOTES! THEY'RE ALL THERE! GO LOOK! PLEASE DON'T KILL ME!

PHOOEY.
WELL, IT'S 7:00. WE GOT TO STAY UP A HALF-HOUR LATER THAN USUAL.
WATTERSON

ROSALYN? WE'RE HOME.

HI, ROSALYN. DID YOU HAVE A QUIET EVENING? DID YOU GET YOUR STUDYING DONE?

...NO, HUH?
I'M SORRY, BUT TONIGHT IS REALLY GOING TO COST YOU.

YOU'RE SURE NO ONE ELSE IN THIS TOWN WILL AGREE TO BABY-SIT CALVIN?
MAYBE YOU WOULD LIKE TO SPEND A WEEK ON THE PHONE!

Calvin and Hobbes by WATTERSON

HERE WE ARE, POISED ON THE PRECIPICE OF "SUICIDE SLOPE." BELOW US LIE THE SKELETAL REMAINS OF HUNDREDS OF LITTLE SLED RIDERS.

SEARCHING FOR THAT ULTIMATE ADRENALINE RUSH, WE PREPARE TO HURL OURSELVES OVER THE BRINK! WHAT FATE AWAITS US?

READY?
NO.

LIFE AND DEATH HANG IN THE BALANCE! A FRACTION OF A SECOND AND ONE WRONG TURN ARE ALL THAT SEPARATE THEM!
THIS ISN'T HELPING.

DAD SAYS THE ANTICIPATION OF HAVING SOMETHING IS OFTEN MORE FUN THAN ACTUALLY HAVING IT.

I THINK HE'S CRAZY. I HATE WAITING FOR THINGS. I LIKE TO HAVE EVERYTHING IMMEDIATELY.

I CAN'T THINK OF ANYTHING I'D RATHER ANTICIPATE THAN HAVE RIGHT AWAY. CAN YOU?

DEATH COMES TO MIND.
I DON'T KNOW WHY I BOTHER TRYING TO HAVE A LITTLE DISCUSSION WITH YOU WHEN YOU'RE ALWAYS SO MORBID.

I WISH SNOW WAS DRY, SO THAT YOU DIDN'T GET ALL COLD AND WET WHEN YOU PLAYED IN IT.

...THEN AGAIN, IF SNOW WAS DRY, YOU COULDN'T PACK IT INTO SNOWBALLS. THAT WOULDN'T BE GOOD.

I WISH IT SNOWED IN SUMMER. WOULDN'T THAT BE FUN? ...WELL NO, ACTUALLY THAT WOULD MAKE IT HARD TO RUN WHEN YOU PLAY BASEBALL.

HECK, IT'S OK JUST THE WAY IT IS.
WE'RE GLAD YOU APPROVE.

YOU CAN ALWAYS TELL WHEN YOU GET TO **OUR** HOUSE.

I THINK OUR SNOW FORTS ARE TOO FAR APART.

POP!

NOW LET'S SEE IF MOM JUMPS OUT OF **HER** SKIN!

CALVIN and HOBBES by WATTERSON

Calvin and Hobbes by WATTERSON

LOOK AT THIS, HOBBES! I COULD ORDER AN OFFICIAL CHOCOLATE FROSTED SUGAR BOMBS BEANIE!

SEE, IT HAS A BATTERY-POWERED PROPELLER ON TOP AND A BIG STAR ON THE FRONT! ISN'T THAT NEAT?

YOU HAVE TO SEND IN FOUR BOX "PROOF OF PURCHASE SEALS" TO GET IT, IT SAYS.
CHOCOLATE FROSTED SUGAR BOMBS

WELL, DON'T JUST STAND THERE, OR THIS'LL TAKE FOREVER.
UGH. THIS STUFF ALWAYS MAKES MY HEART SKIP.
WATTERSON

BLECHH. I FEEL SICK.
OH, C'MON, THAT'S ONLY YOUR SECOND BOWL OF CEREAL.
CHOCOLATE FROSTED SUGAR BOMBS
MILK

THIS STUFF IS PURE SUGAR.
BUT IT'S **FORTIFIED** WITH EIGHT ESSENTIAL VITAMINS, SO IT'S GOOD FOR YOU.
WATTERSON

GIVE ME A BREAK. THIS IS LIKE EATING A BOWL OF MILK DUDS.
LOOK, IT SAYS RIGHT ON THE BOX, "PART OF A WHOLESOME, NUTRITIOUS, BALANCED BREAKFAST."

AND THEY SHOW A GUY EATING FIVE GRAPEFRUITS, A DOZEN BRAN MUFFINS...
YOU KNOW WHY YOU SHAKE LIKE THAT? VITAMIN DEFICIENCY, I'LL BET.

'MORNING, DAD! HOW'S YOUR BREAKFAST?
FINE.

OATMEAL, HUH? A BOWL OF PASTY, BLAND, COLORLESS SLUDGE.
YES. WHY DON'T YOU GO DESCRIBE YOUR **OWN** FOOD SOMEWHERE ELSE?

I'LL BET YOU'D RATHER HAVE A BOWL OF TASTY, LIP-SMACKING, CRUNCHY-ON-THE-OUTSIDE, CHEWY-ON-THE-INSIDE, CHOCOLATE FROSTED SUGAR BOMBS! CAN I POUR YOU SOME?
CHOCOLATE FROSTED SUGAR BOMBS

NO, THANKS. I'M TRYING TO REACH MIDDLE AGE.
WHAT ARE **YOU** HAVING, MOM? BORING OLD TOAST AND TEA?
YOU WANT THE BEANIE, **YOU** EAT THE CEREAL, CALVIN.
WATTERSON

1½ BOXES TO GO, AND I'LL HAVE ENOUGH "PROOF OF PURCHASE SEALS" TO ORDER THE PROPELLER BEANIE THEY OFFER.
CHOCOLATE FROSTED SUGAR BOMBS

CHOCOLATE FROSTED SUGAR BOMBS

1⅓ BOXES TO GO.
MAN, I'M *EARNING* THIS.
CHOCOLATE FROSTED SUGAR BOMBS
WATTERSON

HOBBES, I DID IT! I ATE ENOUGH BOXES OF CEREAL TO GET ALL THE PROOF OF PURCHASE SEALS I NEED!

NOW I CAN ORDER MY BEANIE! OH, BOY! I CAN'T WAIT TO GET IT! I'LL BE SO COOL!

NOT FOR OVER A MONTH. IT SAYS TO ALLOW SIX WEEKS FOR DELIVERY.
SIX WEEKS ?!?

I'LL BE *OLD* THEN!
AND I'M SURE YOUR BEANIE WILL BE THE TALK OF THE REST HOME.
WATTERSON

SCHOOL

MOM! MOM! DID MY BEANIE COME IN THE MAIL?
ARE YOU KIDDING? I JUST MAILED YOUR ORDER THIS MORNING.

I'M NEVER GOING TO MAKE IT SIX WEEKS.
WATTERSON

GOSH, I CAN'T WAIT TO GET MY BEANIE! I HOPE IT COMES SOON. DO YOU THINK IT WILL? IT'S PROBABLY BEEN ALMOST SIX WEEKS BY **NOW**, DON'T YOU THINK?

I ORDERED THE RED BEANIE. BUT WHAT IF IT'S NOT IN STOCK? SHOULD I TAKE THE BLUE ONE, OR WAIT FOR THEM TO REORDER? A BLUE ONE WOULD BE OK, I GUESS, BUT I SURE HOPE THEY HAVE A RED ONE.

I'VE ALWAYS WANTED A BEANIE LIKE THIS, WITH A PROPELLER. BOY, IT'LL BE SO COOL WHEN I HAVE IT. I CAN'T WAIT. WOW! A RED BEANIE! ...OR A BLUE ONE. DO YOU THINK IT WILL COME TOMORROW? DO YOU?

IT HAD SURE BETTER.
YEAH, THAT'S HOW I FEEL, TOO.

THBBPTBTHP

THBBPTHPPTH

HOW WAS SCHOOL TODAY?
OH, IT WAS A BLAST! ...DID MY BEANIE COME TODAY?

PLEASE LET MY BEANIE COME TODAY! I PROMISE I WON'T EVER BE BAD AGAIN! I'LL DO WHATEVER YOU WANT!

PLEASE, PLEASE, PLEASE! I'LL NEVER ASK ANOTHER FAVOR IF TODAY'S THE DAY I GET MY BEANIE!

DID I GET MY BEANIE?
NOPE.

WHAT'S IT TAKE, HUH?!

I CAN'T BELIEVE THIS. EVERY DAY I GET ALL MY HOPES UP, THINKING MY BEANIE WILL COME... AND THEN IT DOESN'T.

AND FOR EACH DAY THAT GOES BY, I FIGURE THE ODDS ARE BETTER THAT IT WILL COME THE *NEXT* DAY, SO MY HOPES GET HIGHER AND HIGHER BEFORE THEY FALL.
IT'S AWFUL.

BUT I'VE BEEN DISAPPOINTED SO OFTEN NOW, I'M FINALLY GETTING NUMB TO IT.
MAYBE THE MAILMAN MADE A SECOND TRIP TODAY AND DELIVERED IT IN THE LAST FIVE MINUTES.

WOW! I NEVER THOUGHT OF THAT! C'MON!
HE'S NOT NUMB.
WATTERSON

THE LONGER YOU WAIT FOR THE MAIL, THE LESS THERE IS IN IT.
WATTERSON

I'M HOME. I DIDN'T GET MY PROPELLER BEANIE TODAY, DID I?

AS A MATTER OF FACT, YOU DID!
IT'S HERE!
HA HA! IT TOOK WEEKS AND WEEKS OF WAITING, BUT AT LONG LAST IT'S HERE! NOW I FINALLY, *FINALLY* GET TO PUT IT ON!

"SOME ASSEMBLY REQUIRED. BATTERIES NOT INCLUDED."
WATTERSON

CAN YOU BELIEVE THIS? I'VE GOT TO ASSEMBLE MY BEANIE PROPELLER AND MOTOR MYSELF!

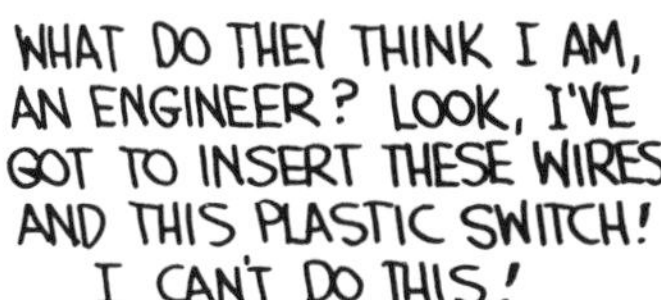
WHAT DO THEY THINK I AM, AN ENGINEER? LOOK, I'VE GOT TO INSERT THESE WIRES AND THIS PLASTIC SWITCH! I CAN'T DO THIS!

HERE, LET ME TRY.
NO! GET AWAY! I'LL DO IT! YOU'D PROBABLY GOOF IT ALL UP, OR...

SNAP
OH NO!
SEE? INSULT A TIGER AND YOU GET BAD LUCK! EVERY TIME!

MY MOTOR BROKE! THE PIECE SNAPPED! NOW MY BEANIE PROPELLER WON'T WORK!!

AAGHHGHHH! I WAITED WEEKS FOR THIS AND NOW IT'S BROKEN, AND I DIDN'T EVEN GET TO WEAR IT!
STUPID ROTTEN PIECE OF LOUSY JUNK!!

IT'S ALL YOUR FAULT! RRGHH GHHGH!
MY FAULT?! I WAS JUST SITTING HERE! YOU BROKE IT!

YOU WILLED ME TO BREAK IT! YOU DID SOME SUBLIMINAL THING! DON'T DENY IT! I KNOW YOU DID! YOU MUST HAVE!
OK, NOW I'M WILLING YOU TO GO JUMP IN THE SEPTIC TANK.

WHAT ARE YOU MAD AT ME FOR?!
GET AWAY FROM ME! I DON'T EVEN WANT TO TALK TO YOU!

YOU BROKE YOUR BEANIE MOTOR, NOT ME! I DIDN'T DO ANYTHING!
YOU DISTRACTED ME!

I DID NOT! I WAS JUST SITTING HERE! YOU BROKE IT ALL BY YOURSELF!
SNIFF *SNIFFLE* ...ALL RIGHT.. I KNOW..

BUT CONSIDERING MY LIFE'S IN SHAMBLES RIGHT NOW, COULDN'T YOU AT LEAST TAKE THE BLAME?

WHAT A RIP-OFF! I ATE ALL THAT CEREAL, WAITED WEEKS AND WEEKS TO GET THE BEANIE, ASSEMBLED IT MYSELF, AND THE DUMB THING DOESN'T EVEN FLY!

Calvin and HOBBES
by WATTERSON
TIGERS DON'T WORRY ABOUT MUCH, DO THEY?
NOPE.
PLOONK

THAT'S ONE OF THE PERKS OF BEING FERAL.

I'M NOT HAVING ENOUGH FUN RIGHT NOW.
YOU'RE NOT?
I'M JUST HAVING A LITTLE BIT OF FUN. I SHOULD BE HAVING LOTS OF FUN.

IT'S SUNDAY. I'VE JUST GOT A FEW PRECIOUS HOURS OF FREEDOM LEFT BEFORE I HAVE TO GO TO SCHOOL TOMORROW.

BETWEEN NOW AND BEDTIME, I HAVE TO SQUEEZE ALL THE FUN POSSIBLE OUT OF EVERY MINUTE! I DON'T WANT TO WASTE A SECOND OF LIBERTY!

EACH MOMENT I SHOULD BE ABLE TO SAY, "I'M HAVING THE TIME OF MY LIFE RIGHT NOW!"

BUT HERE I AM, AND I'M NOT HAVING THE TIME OF MY LIFE! VALUABLE MINUTES ARE DISAPPEARING FOREVER, EVEN AS WE SPEAK! WE'VE GOT TO HAVE MORE FUN! C'MON!

I DIDN'T REALIZE FUN WAS SO MUCH WORK.
SURE! WHEN YOU'RE SERIOUS ABOUT HAVING FUN, IT'S NOT MUCH FUN AT ALL!
WATTERSON

C'MON, CALVIN! THIS IS THE THIRD TIME I'VE CALLED YOU. GET UP.

I DON'T WANT TO GET UP. I DON'T WANT TO GO TO SCHOOL.
WELL, YOU **HAVE** TO, WHETHER YOU WANT TO OR NOT, SO LET'S MOVE.
WATTERSON

FOR YOUR INFORMATION, I DON'T **HAVE** TO DO ANYTHING I DON'T **WANT** TO DO.
IS THAT SO?

SHE SURE CAN MAKE SOMEONE WANT TO DO SOMETHING.

I DON'T WANT TO CATCH THE BUS. I DON'T WANT TO GO TO SCHOOL. I DON'T WANT TO BE HERE AT ALL.

I'M SICK OF EVERYONE TELLING ME WHAT TO DO ALL THE TIME! I HATE MY LIFE! I HATE EVERYTHING! I WISH I WAS **DEAD!**

... WELL, NO, I DON'T. NOT REALLY.

I WISH EVERYONE **ELSE** WAS DEAD.
WATTERSON

HI, CALVIN.
HMPH.

OH, **YOU'RE** REAL PLEASANT THIS MORNING. WHAT'S THE MATTER WITH YOU?
GO STEP IN FRONT OF A CEMENT MIXER, OK?

WHAT A PILL YOU ARE! WHAT A JERK! WELL, WHO NEEDS **YOU?!** YOU CAN JUST STAND THERE AND BE GRUMPY ALL BY YOURSELF!

HMPH.
NOTHING HELPS A BAD MOOD LIKE SPREADING IT AROUND.
WATTERSON

HOW COULD YOU HAVE POSSIBLY FORGOTTEN IT, ANYWAY?! IT'S ALL THE CLASS HAS BEEN DOING! WHERE HAVE YOU BEEN?? DON'T YOU PAY ATTENTION?!

PHOOEY. NO BUGS IN THE BUS WINDOW.
I CAN'T BELIEVE YOU'RE DOING THIS.
CHOOL DISTRI

HEY, ASK THAT KID IF HE'S GOT ANY BUGS IN *HIS* WINDOW.
CALVIN, THERE IS NO WAY YOU'RE GOING TO COMPLETE AN INSECT COLLECTION ON THE WAY TO SCHOOL! FORGET IT!

SIGHHH... WELL, MAYBE YOU'RE RIGHT.

HOW MUCH DO YOU WANT FOR *YOUR* COLLECTION? I'LL GIVE YOU A QUARTER...OR HERE, 30 CENTS.
I SPENT A MONTH ON THIS!

HEY, HERE'S A WORM! WORMS ARE BUGS, AREN'T THEY?
EWW GROSS, CALVIN! THAT'S BEEN FLOATING IN A PUDDLE FOR DAYS.

CLASS DOESN'T START FOR 10 MINUTES. IF I CAN CATCH FIVE BUGS A MINUTE, I'LL GET AN "A" ON MY COLLECTION. SEE, I'M OFF TO A GOOD START.

FIVE BUGS A MINUTE?! YOU'RE OUT OF YOUR MIND.
HERE'S ANOTHER ALREADY.

THAT'S A LITTLE BALL OF LINT!
LIKE I'M SURE THE TEACHER'S GOING TO LOOK **REAL CLOSE** AT EVERY HAIRY BUG IN 30 KIDS' COLLECTIONS!

RINNGGGG
THERE'S THE BELL. WE'VE GOT TO GO TO CLASS.
RATS. I DIDN'T GET 50 BUGS YET.

WHAT DO YOU HAVE?
ONE DROWNED WORM, A PIECE OF FUZZY LINT THAT *LOOKS* LIKE A BUG, A LIVE ANT, AND A SMASHED FLY.

WELL, IF YOU LABEL THEM SCIENTIFICALLY IN THE NEXT 30 SECONDS, MAYBE YOU'LL GET AN "F+."
WE'VE GOT TO **LABEL** THESE *TOO*?!? I WAS JUST GOING TO PUT THEM ALL IN AN ENVELOPE.

ACTUALLY, I DON'T THINK THERE'S ANY WAY YOU'LL GET AN "F+."
FOR ALL THIS WORK, I'D BETTER AT LEAST GET A "D."

Hey Susie,
How's the view way up there? Ha! Ha!
Calvin
P.S. try to steal a chalkboard eraser for me.

PSST... HERE!

HEY SUSIE,
ROSES ARE RED,
A DEEP CRIMSON HUE.
WHEN YOU GOT IN TROUBLE,
YOU SURE WERE TOO!
HA! HA!
CALVIN
!

Calvin, you dirty, rotten, lousy, stinking, nasty piece of moldy scum!!! Drop dead! I hope you...

WRITING NOTES IN CLASS NOW, ARE WE, SUSIE?
HEY, LOOK! SHE'S TURNING RED AGAIN!
EEP!

OH NO, HOW CAN THIS BE HAPPENING?? I'VE BEEN SENT TO SEE THE PRINCIPAL! THIS IS ALL CALVIN'S FAULT! HE'S THE ONE WHO GOT ME IN ALL THIS TROUBLE!

I'M SO SCARED! WHAT AM I GOING TO DO??

I THINK THEY MAKE THE HALL TO THE PRINCIPAL'S OFFICE THIS BIG ON PURPOSE.

WOW, SUSIE GOT SENT TO THE PRINCIPAL'S OFFICE! SHE'S IN TROUBLE NOW, ALL RIGHT!

WHEWW I SURE WAS LUCKY THE TEACHER BLAMED SUSIE FOR EVERYTHING. WHAT A BREAK!

OH, NO! WHAT IF SUSIE RATS ON ME!? SUPPOSE THEY MAKE HER SING! SUPPOSE SHE SQUEALS! SUPPOSE SHE FINGERS ME!

OH, I'M SO RELIEVED. I WAS AFRAID YOU WOULDN'T BELIEVE ME.
OH, YES, WE'VE GOT QUITE A FILE ON OUR FRIEND CALVIN.

THEN I GOT IN TROUBLE WHEN I TOLD MOM, AND THEN I GOT IN TROUBLE AGAIN WHEN SHE TOLD DAD! I'VE BEEN IN HOT WATER EVER SINCE I GOT UP!

Calvin and Hobbes

by Watterson

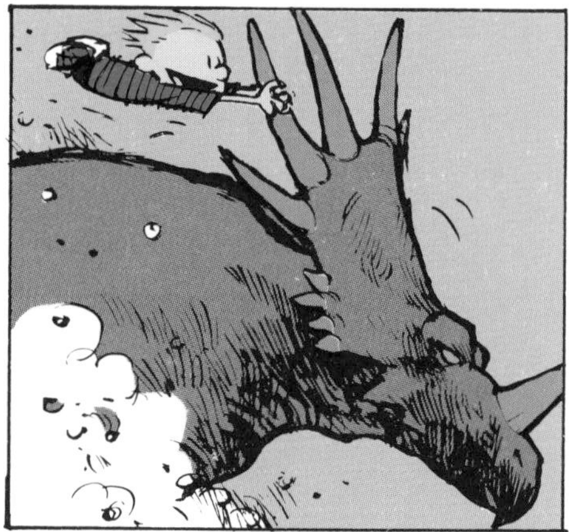

GOTCHA!!

!

HEY! JUST WHAT DO YOU THINK YOU'RE DOING BACK DOWN HERE?!
YOU DIDN'T READ ME MY RIGHTS.

DAD! DAD! OUTER SPACE ALIENS JUST LANDED IN THE BACK YARD!

OH, REALLY. WHAT DO THEY LOOK LIKE?
SORT OF LIKE BIG BAKED POTATOES WITH LASER GUNS. I THINK WE SHOULD DO WHAT THEY SAY.

DID THEY SAY WHAT THEY WANT?
YEAH, THEY WANT 10 DOLLARS.

I'LL BET THEY DO.
SINCE YOU'RE SO BUSY, YOU CAN JUST GIVE THE MONEY TO ME, AND I'LL TAKE IT OVER TO THEM.

Calvin and Hobbes
by WATTERSON
GET UP, CALVIN! I'M NOT GOING TO CALL YOU AGAIN!

I BET.

YOU'RE GOING TO MISS THE BUS! NOW GET OUT OF BED!

YOU DON'T KNOW THE ANSWER? THEN SIT DOWN.
12
- 7

Hey, Twinky, want to see if there's an afterlife?

NO, YOU CAN'T GO PLAY UNTIL YOU FINISH YOUR HOMEWORK.

JUST EAT YOUR FOOD. YOU DON'T NEED TO PLAY WITH IT.

STOP STALLING AND GET IN THE BATHTUB.

NO, YOU CAN'T STAY UP A LITTLE LONGER. GO TO BED.

HAVE A GOOD NIGHT'S SLEEP. TOMORROW'S ANOTHER BIG DAY!

... SIGHHHHHH ...
WATTERSON

HOW COME **YOU** ALWAYS READ ME MY BEDTIME STORY AND NOT MOM?

BECAUSE READING THE BEDTIME STORY IS THE ***DAD'S*** JOB.

AND IT APPEARS TO BE THE ***ONLY*** "DAD'S JOB" AROUND HERE!

LEFT THE DISHES FOR MOM AGAIN, HUH?
TONIGHT'S STORY IS CALLED, "WHY PRINCE CHARMING STAYED SINGLE."
PRINCE ***WHAT***?

I'VE BEEN THINKING. SUPPOSE I GROW UP TO BE ONE OF THE WORLD'S GREATEST MEN OF ALL TIME. SUPPOSE MY NAME WILL BE AN INSPIRATION TO HUMANITY FOR EONS TO COME!

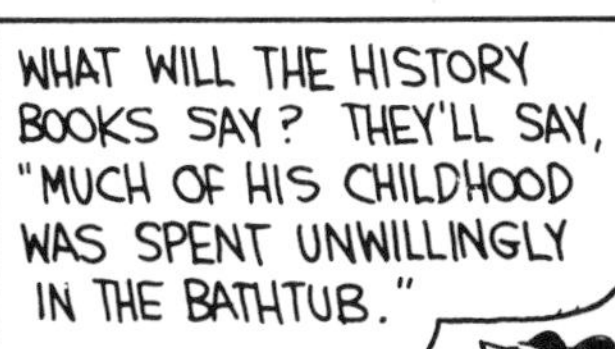
WHAT WILL THE HISTORY BOOKS SAY? THEY'LL SAY, "MUCH OF HIS CHILDHOOD WAS SPENT UNWILLINGLY IN THE BATHTUB."

WHAT AN INDIGNITY THIS BATH IS! IS THIS SITUATION WORTHY OF ONE OF THE GREATEST MEN OF ALL TIME?!?

MY LIKELY HISTORICAL SIGNIFICANCE IS A TERRIBLE BURDEN.
WOULD YOU RATHER THEY SAID YOUR CHILDHOOD WAS DIRTY AND SMELLY?

NNNGKGKK

HOCCHHHH

PTOOEY!

BOY, THEY SURE GO FARTHER WHEN YOU MAKE 'EM RIGHT!
LET'S MAKE UP A ***NEW*** CONTEST, OK?

Calvin and HOBBES

by WATTERSON

HIC
HIC
HIC

(HIC) I HAVE (HIC) HAVE (HIC) I (HIC) I HAVE THE (HIC) THE (HIC)...

THE HIC (HIC) THE (HIC)
WHAT IS IT? WHAT DO YOU HAVE? A DOLLAR?? A NEW COMIC BOOK? WHAT??

THE (HIC HIC) I HAVE (HIC) HAVE THE (HIC) THE (HIC) THE HIC (HIC) THE (HIC)...
I LOVE DOING THIS.

HELP ME (HIC) GET (HIC) RID OF (HIC) THESE DARN (HIC) HIC (HIC) HICCUPS!
HOW?

(HIC) SCARE ME.
OK...

OUR OCEANS ARE FILLED WITH GARBAGE, WE'VE CREATED A HOLE IN THE OZONE THAT'S FRYING THE PLANET, NUCLEAR WASTE IS PILING UP WITHOUT ANY SAFE WAY TO GET RID OF IT ....

(HIC) I MEAN, SURPRISE ME (HIC).
THAT DOESN'T?! BOY, YOU'RE CYNICAL.

HERE. DRINKING FROM THE FAR SIDE OF A GLASS IS SUPPOSED TO CURE HICCUPS.

THE (HIC) FAR SIDE OF (HIC) THE GLASS? (HIC) HOW DO I (HIC) DO THAT?

YOU HAVE TO BEND YOUR HEAD WAY OVER.
OH (HIC) I SEE.

(HIC) THANKS. NOW I'VE GOT THE HICCUPS AND WATER UP MY NOSE.
I THINK MOST HICCUP CURES WERE REALLY INVENTED FOR THE AMUSEMENT OF THE PATIENT'S FRIENDS.

THESE (HIC) HICCUPS ARE DRIVING ME (HIC) CRAZY.

EAT A SPOONFUL OF SUGAR. THAT'S SUPPOSED TO HELP.
I'LL (HIC) TRY ANY-THING.
SU

CRUNCH SMACK SMACK
SUG

WELL? ARE YOU CURED?
(HIC) NOPE. I'D BETTER (HIC) EAT SOME MORE.
GAR
WATTERSON

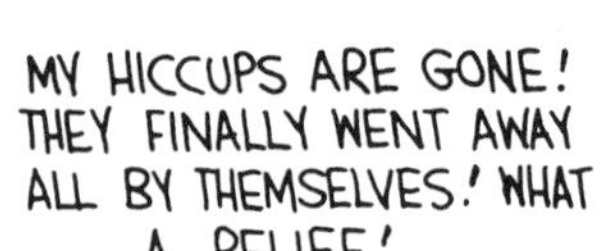
MY HICCUPS ARE GONE! THEY FINALLY WENT AWAY ALL BY THEMSELVES! WHAT A RELIEF!

AAUGHH!

DID I SCARE YOU? DID I CURE YOUR HICCUPS?
GAR
HIC HIC HIC HIC HIC HIC HIC HIC HIC HIC HIC
WATTERSON

LOOK, CALVIN, I BROUGHT HOME SOME JELLY DOUGHNUTS. WOULD YOU LIKE ONE?

NO, JELLY DOUGHNUTS GROSS ME OUT. THEY'RE LIKE EATING GIANT, SQUISHY BUGS. YOU BITE INTO THEM AND ALL THEIR PURPLE GUTS SPILL OUT THE OTHER END.

YOU CAN EAT THEM.

MY FRIENDS ASK ME HOW I STAY THIN.
WATTERSON

Calvin and Hobbes
by WATTERSON
WHENEVER I NEED TO DO SOME SERIOUS THINKING, I GO FOR A WALK IN THE WOODS.

THERE ARE ALWAYS A MILLION DISTRACTIONS OUT HERE.

I DON'T BELIEVE IN ETHICS ANY MORE.

AS FAR AS I'M CONCERNED, THE ENDS JUSTIFY THE MEANS.

GET WHAT YOU CAN WHILE THE GETTING'S GOOD – THAT'S WHAT I SAY! MIGHT MAKES RIGHT! THE WINNERS WRITE THE HISTORY BOOKS!

IT'S A DOG-EAT-DOG WORLD, SO I'LL DO WHATEVER I HAVE TO, AND LET OTHERS ARGUE ABOUT WHETHER IT'S "RIGHT" OR NOT.

HEYY!
SHOVE!

WHY'D YOU DO THAT?!?
YOU WERE IN MY WAY. NOW YOU'RE NOT. THE ENDS JUSTIFY THE MEANS.

I DIDN'T MEAN FOR EVERYONE, YOU DOLT! JUST ME!
AHH...
WATTERSON

Calvin and Hobbes

by WATTERSON

COME ON, CALVIN! WE WERE SUPPOSED TO HAVE LEFT A HALF-HOUR AGO.

WHERE ARE WE GOING?
FOR THE HUNDREDTH TIME, WE'RE GOING TO A WEDDING. NOW GET IN THE CAR. YOUR DAD'S WAITING.

BUT WHAT IF I FORGOT SOMETHING?
WE'RE ONLY GOING TO BE GONE OVERNIGHT. YOU'LL GET BY.
WATTERSON

TURN AROUND! WE FORGOT HOBBES! STOP THE CAR!

WE CAN'T TURN AROUND, CALVIN. WE'RE LATE ALREADY.
BUT DA-AD!!

YOU COULD'VE BEEN READY ON TIME AND HAD ALL YOUR THINGS TOGETHER, BUT YOU PUT UP A FUSS ABOUT GOING, MADE US LATE, AND YOU FORGOT YOUR TIGER. IT'S YOUR OWN FAULT.

YOU'D TURN AROUND IF WE'D FORGOTTEN MOM!
THAT'S BECAUSE SHE'S THE ONLY ONE WHO KNOWS WHERE THIS PLACE IS.
HAR HAR.
WATTERSON

WHEN IS THIS DUMB WEDDING GOING TO BE OVER?! I DON'T EVEN KNOW THESE PEOPLE.

THIS WOULD BE A LOT MORE FUN IF HOBBES WAS HERE. I CAN'T BELIEVE WE LEFT HIM AT HOME.

I HOPE HE'S OK. WHAT'S HE GOING TO EAT? WE DIDN'T LEAVE ANY FOOD OUT, AND WE'LL BE GONE ALMOST TWO WHOLE DAYS! HOBBES WILL BE STARVING!
WATTERSON

I THINK I'LL LET DAD GO INTO THE HOUSE FIRST.

HEY, MOM, HOW DO YOU MAKE A LONG-DISTANCE CALL FROM OUR MOTEL ROOM?

DON'T PLAY WITH THE PHONE, CALVIN. WHO ON EARTH DO YOU WANT TO CALL?
HOBBES. I WANT TO MAKE SURE HE'S OK.

HOBBES ISN'T GOING TO ANSWER THE PHONE. DON'T BE SILLY. YOU'LL SEE HIM TOMORROW.
BUT HE'S PROBABLY ALL LONELY!

I'M SURE HE'S HAVING A GOOD TIME.
I HOPE HE ISN'T RENTING SOME MOVIE THAT I WANTED TO SEE.
WATTERSON

MOM, I CAN'T SLEEP.

I'M SURE YOU CAN IF YOU JUST LIE QUIETLY.
BUT HOBBES ISN'T HERE.

TIGERS ARE VERY COMFORTING. I ALWAYS FALL RIGHT ASLEEP WHEN I LISTEN TO HOBBES BREATHING.

WELL, YOU CAN LISTEN TO YOUR DAD SNORING.
THAT'S DAD? I THOUGHT THOSE WERE TRUCKS DOWN-SHIFTING ON THE HIGHWAY.
WATTERSON

WELL, WE'RE FINALLY HOME!
HOORAYY! NOW I GET TO SEE HOBBES!

BOY, I DIDN'T THINK WE'D EVER GET HOME. THE WHOLE TRIP WAS ONE LONG COMPLAINT ABOUT LEAVING HOBBES BEHIND.
NEXT TIME WE SHOULD TAKE THE TIGER AND FORGET THE KID.

GOSH, IT'S DRAFTY IN HERE...
THE WINDOW'S SMASHED! LOOK AT THE GLASS!

SOMEBODY BROKE IN!!
HOBBES! FIND HOBBES!

I TOLD MOM AND DAD WE LEFT HOBBES BEHIND.... I TRIED TO GET THEM TO TURN AROUND AND COME BACK.... AND NOW LOOK, HOBBES WAS ALL ALONE WHEN OUR HOUSE WAS BROKEN INTO!

HOBBES? ARE YOU DOWN HERE? YOU'VE GOT TO BE SOMEWHERE!

HERE HE IS, CALVIN! I FOUND HOBBES!

YOU FOUND HIM! IS HE OK?? HE'S NOT HURT, IS HE?
HE'S FINE. HE WAS UNDER THE BED COVERS.
WATTERSON

HOBBES, I'M SO GLAD TO SEE YOU!! YOU'RE SAFE AND SOUND! (SNIFF) AND NOW I AM, TOO!
IT LOOKS LIKE WE'RE A WHOLE FAMILY AGAIN.
SUCH AS IT IS, YES.

...AND THE TELEVISION'S GONE, TOO.
DO YOU HAPPEN TO HAVE THE SERIAL NUMBER?

I'LL BET THE BURGLARS GOT SCARED OFF WHEN THEY SAW THERE WAS A TIGER IN THE HOUSE! HOBBES WAS HERE THE WHOLE TIME!
CALVIN, NOT NOW, OK? I'M BUSY.

NOBODY STICKS AROUND LONG WHEN HE SEES A TIGER, THAT'S FOR SURE! MANDIBLES OF DEATH, THAT'S WHAT HOBBES HAS!
RIGHT. WHY DON'T YOU GO TELL YOUR MOM?

MAYBE HOBBES SHOULD LOOK AT SOME MUG SHOTS. CAN WE GO TO THE STATION AND IDENTIFY SUSPECTS? HUH, CAN WE?
DEAR!
I SURE MEET THE WEIRDOS IN THIS JOB..

I'VE SWEPT UP MOST OF THE GLASS FROM THE WINDOW.
OK, I'LL GET SOMETHING TO COVER UP THE HOLE.

DO YOU THINK IT'S SAFE TO STAY HERE TONIGHT? SUPPOSE THE BURGLARS COME BACK!
THE POLICE SAID THEY'D DRIVE BY, AND WE'LL LEAVE LOTS OF LIGHTS ON.

UGH, IT'S SO CREEPY KNOWING THESE GOONS HAVE BEEN IN OUR HOUSE. I DON'T FEEL SAFE AT ALL.
I KNOW. AND THIS MUST REALLY BE SCARY FOR A LITTLE KID LIKE CALVIN.

GOSH, I CAN'T WAIT TO TELL EVERYONE AT SCHOOL HOW OUR HOUSE GOT ROBBED!
BE SURE TO SAY WHO SCARED THE BURGLARS AWAY AFTER THEY TOOK THE TV AND JEWELRY.
WATTERSON

A MAN'S HOME IS HIS CASTLE, BUT IT SHOULDN'T HAVE TO BE A FORTRESS.

I FIGURED THAT ONCE YOU GREW UP, YOU AUTOMATICALLY KNEW WHAT TO DO IN ANY GIVEN SCENARIO.

I DON'T THINK I'D HAVE BEEN IN SUCH A HURRY TO REACH ADULTHOOD IF I'D KNOWN THE WHOLE THING WAS GOING TO BE AD-LIBBED.

WELL, AT LEAST WE WEREN'T HOME WHEN OUR HOUSE WAS BROKEN INTO. NO ONE WAS HURT. WE'RE ALL TOGETHER AND OK.

WE LOST A FEW OF OUR NICE THINGS, BUT THINGS DON'T MATTER MUCH REALLY.

IT'S HARD TO BELIEVE HOW OFTEN WE FORGET THAT.
WATTERSON

CAN I BE EXCUSED NOW?
YOU DIDN'T FINISH YOUR DINNER.

WELL, I DIDN'T LIKE IT VERY MUCH, AND THERE'S THIS TV SHOW I WANT TO WATCH, SO...
OUR TV WAS STOLEN, REMEMBER?

WATTERSON

GOSH, I GUESS I'LL EAT MY ASPARAGUS, DO MY HOMEWORK, AND GO STRAIGHT TO BED, THEN.
AND WE'RE SO PROUD OF HOW YOU HANDLE ADVERSITY.

THIS IS WHERE OUR TELEVISION USED TO BE.

BUT WE DON'T HAVE A TV ANYMORE. NOW WE HAVE A BLANK WALL TO WATCH.

SO HERE I AM, NOT BEING ENTERTAINED.

A POINTLESS EXISTENCE, HUH?
I MEAN, THE WALL IS EVEN PLAIN OLD *WHITE*!
WATTERSON

Calvin and HOBBES

by WATTERSON

GOOD NEWS, HOBBES! I'M STARTING A SECRET CLUB, AND YOU CAN BE IN IT!
OH, BOY!

IT'LL BE GREAT! WE'LL THINK OF SECRET NAMES FOR OURSELVES, SECRET CODES FOR OUR SECRET CORRESPONDENCE, A SECRET HANDSHAKE, ...

WE'LL HAVE A SECRET CLUB-HOUSE WITH A SECRET KNOCK TO GET IN, AND WE'LL DO BIG, SECRETIVE THINGS!
WHY ALL THE SECRECY?

PEOPLE PAY MORE ATTENTION TO YOU WHEN THEY THINK YOU'RE UP TO SOMETHING.

OK, THE FIRST THING WE NEED IS A NAME FOR OUR SECRET CLUB.

LET'S CALL IT "THE HOBBES FAN CLUB"!
THE HOBBES FAN CLUB?! GIVE ME A BREAK! I'M SURE!!

THIS IS A TOP-SECRET SOCIETY! THE NAME SHOULD BE SOMETHING MYSTERIOUS! SOMETHING VAGUELY OMINOUS AND CHILLING!

SOMETHING LIKE, "THE SINISTER ICY BLACK HAND OF DEATH CLUB"!
I STILL LIKE MY IDEA BETTER.

I'VE GOT IT! WE'LL CALL OUR CLUB G.R.O.S.S. - GET RID OF SLIMY GIRLS! THAT WAY, SUSIE DERKINS CAN'T JOIN!

IS SHE SLIMY?
ALL GIRLS ARE SLIMY. NOW THE FIRST ORDER OF BUSINESS IS TO ELECT OFFICERS.

I GET TO BE PRESIDENT! I GET TO BE PRESIDENT!
OH, NO YOU DON'T! THIS WHOLE CLUB WAS MY IDEA, SO I GET TO BE PRESIDENT.

OK, THEN I GET TO BE KING AND TYRANT.
HEY, NO! THAT'S WHAT I WANT TO BE! YOU CAN BE PRESIDENT!

HI, CALVIN! WHAT ARE YOU DOING, MAKING PAPER HATS? CAN I MAKE ONE, TOO?

DON'T BE RIDICULOUS. THIS IS THE OFFICIAL CHAPEAU OF OUR TOP-SECRET CLUB, G.R.O.S.S. – GET RID OF SLIMY GIRLS!

"SLIMY GIRLS"?!
I KNOW THAT'S REDUNDANT, BUT OTHERWISE IT DOESN'T SPELL ANYTHING. NOW GO AWAY.

GIRLS AREN'T SLIMY!
DON'T GET GUNK ON ME. I TOOK A BATH LAST SATURDAY AND I'M ALL CLEAN.

I CAN'T BELIEVE YOU STARTED A SECRET CLUB JUST TO EXCLUDE GIRLS! THERE'S NOTHING WRONG WITH GIRLS!
SEE, HOBBES? GIRLS ARE SO EMOTIONAL.

YOU'RE THE MEANEST, MOST ROTTEN LITTLE KID I KNOW! WELL, FINE! PLAY WITH YOUR STUFFED TIGER! SEE WHAT I CARE! I DON'T WANT TO PLAY WITH A STINKER LIKE YOU ANYWAY!!

WOW, WHAT A GREAT CLUB!

OK, WE'VE GOT A SIGN FOR OUR SECRET CLUB, SO NOW WE NEED TO FIND A SECRET MEETING PLACE.
G.R.O.S.S.

I KNOW! WE CAN SET UP A CARD TABLE IN THE GARAGE! THAT WOULD BE PERFECT FOR DRAWING UP MAPS AND STUFF!

HMM, THERE'S NOT MUCH ROOM WITH THE CAR HERE. LET'S PUSH IT INTO THE DRIVE.
SHOULDN'T YOU ASK YOUR MOM TO MOVE IT INSTEAD?

NAHH. SHE WON'T CARE IF WE PUSH IT OUT. C'MON.
IN THE PAST, YOU'VE BEEN A REMARKABLY POOR JUDGE OF WHAT YOUR MOM CARES ABOUT.

HELP ME PUSH THE CAR OUT OF THE GARAGE. I CAN'T BUDGE IT BY MYSELF.

I STILL THINK YOU SHOULD ASK YOUR MOM TO MOVE IT.
THEN SHE'D PROBABLY SAY NO, AND WE WON'T HAVE THE GARAGE FOR OUR CLUBHOUSE!

BUT IF WE **DON'T** ASK HER, WE'LL GET IN TROUBLE.
WE WON'T GET IN TROUBLE!

EVERY TIME YOU SAY THAT, WE DO.
MOM WOULDN'T CARE ABOUT THESE THINGS IF SHE WOULDN'T KEEP FINDING OUT ABOUT THEM.

LOOK, STOP BEING SUCH A BABY AND HELP ME PUSH THE CAR INTO THE DRIVEWAY. WE'LL MOVE IT 10 FEET. WHAT COULD POSSIBLY GO WRONG?!

WHENEVER YOU ASK THAT, MY TAIL GETS ALL BUSHY.
OH, KNOCK IT OFF. MOM WILL BE GLAD WE DID THIS OURSELVES AND DIDN'T BOTHER HER.

WELL, SHE **DOES** HATE TO BE BOTHERED.
RIGHT. NOW PUSH! PUSH!

HEY, THE CAR'S NOT STOPPING! **STOP! STOP!**
I THINK YOU'RE MOM'S GOING TO BE BOTHERED.

STOP THE CAR! IT'S STILL ROLLING!

THE DRIVEWAY MUST BE SLANTED DOWNHILL!
IT'S GOING FASTER! **WHOA! WHOA!**

JUMP IN AND PULL THE EMERGENCY BRAKE!
I CAN'T CATCH THE DOOR! OH, NO! OH, NO!

IT'S GOING TO GO INTO THE ROAD! DON'T FOLLOW IT!
LOOK OUT! WILD CAR!!

I HAVEN'T SEEN CALVIN FOR ABOUT 15 MINUTES NOW.

THAT PROBABLY MEANS HE'S GETTING IN TROUBLE.
WATTERSON

THE CAR IS ROLLING INTO THE ROAD!!
WHAT IF SOMEONE HITS IT?!?

LOOK OUT! LOOK OUT! THERE'S NO ONE DRIVING!!
THERE IT GOES!!

I CAN'T WATCH!
GRUNTCH

NOBODY HIT IT! IT JUST WENT INTO THE RAVINE ACROSS THE STREET!
HOORAY, WE'RE DEAD.
WATTERSON

OH MAN, OH MAN, OH MAN.

OH MAN.

WHAT DO YOU SUPPOSE A CAR LIKE THIS COSTS? I'LL BET AT *LEAST* $75.
OH *MAN*.
WATTERSON

MY LIFE IS FLASHING BEFORE MY EYES.
YEAH, I DOUBT YOUR PARENTS FIGURED YOU'D WRECK THEIR CAR BEFORE YOU WERE 16.

WHAT ARE WE GOING TO DO?? WE'LL NEVER GET THE CAR OUT OF THE RAVINE.

SHOULD WE ACT SURPRISED, LIKE THE CAR JUST ROLLED HERE BY ITSELF? MAYBE MOM AND DAD WOULD FALL FOR THAT.

OR MAYBE THEY WON'T EVEN NOTICE IF WE JUST DON'T SAY ANYTHING. YOU THINK?

I CAN BE PACKED IN FIVE MINUTES.
OK, I'LL TRY TO GET THE MAPS OUT OF THE GLOVE COMPARTMENT.

HI, MOM! HOBBES AND I ARE BACK! DO I HAVE ANY CLEAN CLOTHES? I MEAN, I'M JUST WONDERING!

I'M GOING TO MAKE MYSELF A FEW DOZEN SANDWICHES! UH... I'M REALLY HUNGRY!

NO NEED TO GET UP, OR LOOK, FOR EXAMPLE, OUT THE WINDOW! JUST STAY WHERE YOU ARE FOR ANOTHER 10 MINUTES!

WHAT'S THE MATTER WITH YOU?
AAUGHH!
HA HA HA HA! NOTHING! UH, WHY DO YOU ASK?!?

I GOT A COUPLE SANDWICHES MADE, BUT I THINK MOM WAS GETTING SUSPICIOUS. ARE YOU PACKED? WE'D BETTER GO!

SHOULD I TAKE THE YO-YO OR THE BUBBLES? ...OR BOTH?
HOBBES, COME ON! WE'LL BE LUCKY TO GET OUT OF HERE WITH OUR LIVES!

MOM'S BOUND TO LOOK OUTSIDE ANY MINUTE NOW AND SEE THE CAR IN THE DITCH! IF WE'RE NOT IN THE NEXT COUNTY BY THEN, IT'S CURTAINS! LET'S GO!

WHERE'S A FREIGHT TRAIN WHEN YOU REALLY NEED ONE?

POOF POOF POOF POOF POOF

OK, (POOF)... I THINK WE'VE GOT ENOUGH OF A HEAD START. WE CAN REST A MINUTE.

DO YOU THINK YOUR MOM HAS SEEN THE CAR BY NOW?
PROBABLY. SHE'S PROBABLY CALLED DAD AT WORK, AND HE'S PROBABLY ON HIS WAY HOME NOW!

WELL, WE'RE SURELY IN SOME OTHER STATE BY NOW. LET'S STOP HERE.

BOY, IT NEVER ONCE OCCURRED TO ME THAT I'D BE SPENDING THE REST OF MY LIFE ON THE LAM.

SPEAKING OF LAMB, WHAT KIND OF SANDWICHES DID YOU BRING?
HOW CAN YOU THINK OF EATING? I'M SO WORRIED I FEEL SICK.

REALLY? CAN I HAVE YOUR SANDWICH TOO?
SIX YEARS OLD AND A FUGITIVE FROM JUSTICE. I CAN'T BELIEVE IT.

WHAT'S GOING ON, I WONDER. WHY ARE ALL THOSE CARS SLOWING DOWN AS THEY GO BY?

GOSH, DID SOMEONE HAVE AN ACCIDENT? IT LOOKS LIKE THERE'S A CAR IN THE DITCH! ...BUT I DON'T SEE ANYONE BY IT.

AND HOW ON EARTH DID THEY GO IN STRAIGHT BACKWARD? TO DO THAT, THE CAR WOULD'VE HAD TO COME...

...RIGHT...OUT...OUR... DRIVEWAY!
WATTERSON

WELL, MOM'S SURE TO HAVE FOUND THE CAR BY NOW AND GUESSED WHAT WE DID.

NOW I KNOW WHAT THEY MEAN WHEN THEY SAY YOU CAN'T GO HOME AGAIN.
WATTERSON

WHAT'S THAT SOUND?
I DON'T HEAR ANYTHING.

THERE! SOMETHING IS CRASHING THROUGH THE BRUSH!
IT SOUNDS BIG! MAYBE IT'S A BEAR!

THERE ARE *BEARS* OUT HERE ?!?
CLIMB THE TREE! CLIMB THE TREE!
WATTERSON

IF YOU ASK *ME*, TIGERS ARE THE ONLY FEROCIOUS ANIMALS THE WORLD REALLY NEEDS.
"BOY, 6, KILLED BY BEAR! PARENTS SAVED THE TROUBLE."

DO YOU THINK WE'RE SAFE? SHOULD WE CLIMB HIGHER?
IT'S HARD TO SAY WITH BEARS.

THERE IT IS! THE BEAR'S COMING OUT OF THE BRUSH! OH NO! IT LOOKS LIKE IT'S ON ITS HIND LEGS! BEARS STAND UP ONLY WHEN THEY'RE REALLY MAD!!

WAIT, THAT'S NOT A BEAR. THAT'S YOUR MOM!
AAUGHH! EVEN WORSE! CLIMB HIGHER! CLIMB HIGHER!

THERE YOU ARE. COME DOWN SO I CAN TALK TO YOU.
NO. YOU'LL KILL US. WE'RE RUNNING AWAY.

I'M NOT GOING TO KILL YOU. I JUST WANT TO FIND OUT WHAT HAPPENED. ARE YOU OK? WAS ANYONE HURT?
NO ONE WAS HURT. WE WERE PUSHING THE CAR INTO THE DRIVE AND IT KEPT ROLLING.

THE CAR DIDN'T HIT ANYTHING?
IT JUST WENT ACROSS THE ROAD AND INTO THE DITCH. THAT'S WHEN WE TOOK OFF.

WELL, THE TOW TRUCK PULLED IT OUT, AND THERE'S NO DAMAGE, SO YOU CAN COME HOME NOW.
FIRST LET'S HEAR YOU SAY YOU LOVE ME.

BOY, HOBBES, ISN'T IT FUNNY HOW THINGS SOMETIMES WORK OUT? MOM AND DAD SAW RIGHT AWAY THAT WHAT HAPPENED TO THE CAR WAS AN ACCIDENT.

THEY WERE SO RELIEVED NO ONE GOT HURT THAT ALL WE GOT WAS A LECTURE ON SAFETY AND ASKING PERMISSION. THEY DIDN'T EVEN RAISE THEIR VOICES.

PARENTS ARE SURE INSCRUTABLE, HUH? SEND THEIR CAR OVER A DITCH AND YOU DON'T EVEN GET YELLED AT.

...BUT TRY KEEPING LIVE WORMS IN YOUR DAD'S...
LET'S NOT TALK ABOUT THAT, OK?!

Calvin and HOBBES
by WATTERSON
TRUE FRIENDS ARE HARD TO COME BY.

I NEED MORE MONEY.

I WISH PEOPLE WERE MORE LIKE ANIMALS.

ANIMALS DON'T TRY TO CHANGE YOU OR MAKE YOU FIT IN. THEY JUST ENJOY THE PLEASURE OF YOUR COMPANY.

ANIMALS AREN'T CONDITIONAL ABOUT FRIENDSHIPS. ANIMALS LIKE YOU JUST THE WAY YOU ARE.

THEY LISTEN TO YOUR PROBLEMS, THEY COMFORT YOU WHEN YOU'RE SAD, AND ALL THEY ASK IN RETURN IS A LITTLE KINDNESS.

WHOOONK!
SOB IT'S SO...SO TRUE!
HOOOOT!
THBPBTPTH!
WATTERSON

... AND SPEAKING OF "A LITTLE KINDNESS," I'D HAVE A TUNA FISH SANDWICH ANY TIME SOON THAT YOU HAPPEN TO MAKE ONE...
OF COURSE, SOME ANIMALS GET ON YOUR NERVES ONCE IN A WHILE.

HERE'S THE LATEST POLL OF HOUSEHOLD 6-YEAR-OLDS, DAD.
AN OVERWHELMING MAJORITY EXPRESS AMAZEMENT AT HOW LITTLE YOU'VE ACCOMPLISHED AS DAD SO FAR. THE IMPRESSION IS THAT YOU'RE AVOIDING ALL THE HARD DECISIONS THAT NEED TO BE MADE.

IN FACT, NONE OF THOSE POLLED COULD NAME A SINGLE INSTANCE OF TRUE PATERNAL LEADERSHIP.

HOW ABOUT IF I LEAD YOU UPSTAIRS TO YOUR BED?
HA HA. IF WE CAN BE SERIOUS FOR A MOMENT, I HAVE SOME INNOVATIVE IDEAS ABOUT MY ALLOWANCE.

LOOK AT ALL THESE ANTS.

THEY'RE ALL RUNNING LIKE MAD, WORKING TIRELESSLY ALL DAY, NEVER STOPPING, NEVER RESTING.

AND FOR WHAT? TO BUILD A TINY LITTLE HILL OF SAND THAT COULD BE WIPED OUT AT ANY MOMENT! ALL THEIR WORK COULD BE FOR NOTHING, AND YET THEY KEEP ON BUILDING. THEY NEVER GIVE UP!

I SUPPOSE THERE'S A LESSON IN THAT.
YEAH ... ANTS ARE MORONS. LET'S SEE WHAT'S ON TV.

BOY, WHAT A GROUCH.

Calvin and Hobbes

by WATTERSON

HI, HOBBES! WHATCHA DOIN'?
NOTHING.

NOTHING AT ALL?
NOPE.

I'LL HELP.
PLEASE DO.

ALIENS WELCOME COME AS YOU ARE!
WHAT WILL YOU DO WHEN YOUR PARENTS SEE THIS?
BY THEN I HOPE TO BE HALFWAY TO THE NEXT GALAXY.

OH, NO! CALVIN HAS TURNED INTO ONE OF HIS OWN CHILDHOOD DRAWINGS!

HIS ANATOMICAL REFERENCES BEING OBSCURE AT BEST, CALVIN FINDS IT DIFFICULT TO MOVE! ARE THESE LOWER APPENDAGES FEET OR WHEELS?

HIS OWN MOM THINKS HE'S SOME KIND OF HELICOPTER! IF ONLY CALVIN HAD LEARNED TO DRAW BETTER!

NO ONE UNDERSTANDS MY WORK.
THAT'S WHAT ALL ARTISTS SAY.

Calvin and Hobbes

by WATTERSON

DEAR MOM,
HOW DO I LOVE YOU?
LET ME COUNT THE WAYS:

WHERE ARE YOU GOING?
OUT.

DID YOU PICK UP YOUR ROOM LIKE I ASKED YOU TO?
NO.

SO WHEN YOU SAY YOU'RE GOING "OUT," YOU REALLY MEAN YOU'RE GOING BACK UPSTAIRS TO CLEAN YOUR ROOM, RIGHT?

ENGLISH MUST NOT BE HER FIRST LANGUAGE.

WHAT ARE YOU DOING DOWN HERE AGAIN? DIDN'T I JUST SEND YOU TO CLEAN YOUR ROOM?!

TWISTED FIEND! NO FOUR WALLS CAN HOLD STUPENDOUS MAN! YOU'VE BEEN FOILED AGAIN, EVIL MOM-LADY! HA HA HA!

OH YEAH?
!

GREAT ZOK! SHE'S FIXED HER MIND-SCRAMBLING EYEBALL RAY ON ME! I'M SUDDENLY FILLED WITH THE DESIRE TO GO BACK UPSTAIRS AND DO HER NEFARIOUS BIDDING!
GLAD TO HEAR IT.

"CLEAN UP YOUR ROOM! CLEAN UP YOUR ROOM!" THAT'S ALL I EVER HEAR!

IT'S MY ROOM, RIGHT?!? IF I DON'T MIND THE MESS, WHAT BUSINESS IS IT OF ANYONE ELSE?! THIS IS TYRANNY! I HATE CLEANING MY ROOM!

IT'S GOING TO TAKE ME ALL DAY TO DO THIS! OOH, THIS MAKES ME MAD! A WHOLE DAY SHOT! WASTED! DOWN THE DRAIN! GONE!
AARGH!

ARE YOU KIDDING? HOW COULD THIS POSSIBLY TAKE ALL DAY?
HECK, IT'LL BE ANOTHER HOUR BEFORE I'M EVEN THROUGH GRIPING.

CLEANING MY ROOM WILL GO A LOT FASTER IF WE **BOTH** WORK, RIGHT?

SO I'LL SIT HERE AND DO ALL THE TEDIOUS, AGONIZING PLANNING AND ORGANIZING...
...YOU KNOW, MAKING THE TOUGH CALLS AND THE HARD DECISIONS. YOU WON'T HAVE TO DO ANY OF THAT.

ALL **YOU** DO THEN IS PICK UP WHAT I TELL YOU TO, OK?

HEY! DID I **SAY** TO PICK UP **ME?!** NO, AS A MATTER OF FACT, I DIDN'T! GET AWAY FROM THAT TRASH CAN! **I'M** THE ORGANIZER! **HEY!**

I CLEANED MY STUPID ROOM! CAN I GO OUTSIDE NOW?!

THAT DIDN'T TAKE YOU VERY LONG. LET'S SEE WHAT KIND OF JOB YOU DID.
I DID A **GREAT** JOB! SEE? CAN I GO NOW?

YOUR ROOM LOOKS GOOD. NOW DID YOU STRAIGHTEN UP YOUR CLOSET LIKE I ASKED YOU TO?
AAUGH! DON'T OPEN THAA...

BACK TO WORK, KIDDO.
YOU MADE **THIS** MESS! **YOU** CLEAN IT UP!

WHACK

OUR FAVORITE GAMES ARE THE ONES WE DON'T UNDERSTAND!
YOU MISSED A WICKET! NO GOAL! NO GOAL!

Calvin and HOBBES
by WATTERSON
BLIPP
SPLOPP
BLOOP
BLIBB

LET'S FACE IT, WE'RE AESTHETES.

HERE COMES SUSIE. JUST IGNORE HER.
HI, CALVIN. CAN I PLAY WITH YOU AND YOUR TIGER?

HOBBES AND I ARE NOT PLAYING. WE'RE DOING BIG IMPORTANT THINGS, AND WE DON'T NEED YOU TO MESS THEM UP.
IT DOESN'T LOOK TO ME LIKE YOU'RE DOING ANYTHING SO IMPORTANT.

WELL WE ARE, SO GO AWAY. WE'VE WASTED TOO MUCH TIME TALKING TO YOU ALREADY.
YOU'RE JUST PLAYING IN THE MUD!

THAT'S JUST WHAT IT LOOKS LIKE TO IGNORANT GIRLS LIKE YOU! GET LOST!
ALL RIGHT, YOU LITTLE CREEP! I DON'T NEED YOU! I'VE GOT BETTER THINGS TO DO THAN SIT IN THE MUD LIKE A PIG!

A PIG?! BY GOLLY, I'LL SHOW YOU!
DON'T BEND OVER! YOUR CURLY PINK TAIL SHOWS! OINK! OINK! OINK! OINK!

EAT SOME MUD, SUSIE!
HA HA! YOU MISSED! OINK! OINK! OINK!

AHHH, SPRING! THAT MAGICAL TIME OF YEAR WHEN A YOUNG MAN'S FANCY TURNS TO LOVE!
SHUT UP.
WATTERSON

Calvin and Hobbes
by WATTERSON
DID YOU WATCH ANY TELEVISION YESTERDAY?
NO.

GOSH, WHAT WAS YESTERDAY LIKE?

I THINK LIFE SHOULD BE MORE LIKE TV.

I THINK ALL OF LIFE'S PROBLEMS OUGHT TO BE SOLVED IN 30 MINUTES WITH SIMPLE HOMILIES, DON'T YOU? I THINK WEIGHT AND ORAL HYGIENE OUGHT TO BE OUR BIGGEST CONCERNS.

I THINK WE SHOULD ALL HAVE POWERFUL, HIGH-PAYING JOBS, AND EVERYONE SHOULD DRIVE FANCY SPORTS CARS. ALL OUR DESIRES SHOULD BE INSTANTLY GRATIFIED.

WOMEN SHOULD ALWAYS WEAR TIGHT CLOTHES, AND MEN SHOULD CARRY POWERFUL HANDGUNS.

LIFE OVERALL SHOULD BE MORE GLAMOROUS, THRILL-PACKED, AND FILLED WITH APPLAUSE, DON'T YOU THINK?

I THINK MY LIFE IS TOO FEATHERBRAINED ALREADY.
OF COURSE, IF LIFE WAS REALLY LIKE THAT, WHAT WOULD WE WATCH ON TV?
WATTERSON

HELP! A BEE! A BEE!
RUN FOR YOUR LIFE!

HOBBES! DID YOU SEE IT?? IT WAS THE BIGGEST BEE IN THE WORLD! IT WAS THE SIZE OF A KAISER ROLL! IT MUST'VE WEIGHED 70 POUNDS!

IT SOUNDED LIKE A HELICOPTER, AND ITS STINGER WAS LIKE A HARPOON! IT MUST'VE BEEN A KILLER DEATH BEE! MAN, I'M LUCKY IT DIDN'T GET ME!

LIFE IN THE GREAT SUBURBAN OUTBACK IS CERTAINLY FRAUGHT WITH PERIL.
IF YOU'D SEEN IT, YOU'D HAVE BEEN SCARED, TOO.

I CAN'T IMAGINE MASTERING THE SKILLS INVOLVED HERE WITHOUT A CLEARER UNDERSTANDING OF WHO'S GOING TO BE IMPRESSED.

I SAW THE MAN IN THE MOON TONIGHT.
MM.

I DIDN'T KNOW THE MOON MADE FACES.
THAT'S "PHASES".

Calvin and Hobbes

by WATTERSON

THE GIANT PTERANODON HOPS TO THE EDGE OF THE CLIFF.

THERE HE SPREADS HIS BAT-LIKE WINGS AND TAKES TO THE AIR! SOARING HIGH OVER THE PREHISTORIC VALLEY, THE PTERANODON IS TRULY A MAJESTIC SIGHT!

THAT'S IT, THINK MAJESTIC!
I'M THINKING WE SHOULD'VE PICKED A SMALLER CLIFF!

IT'S TOO DARN HOT OUT HERE.
YOU COULD GO WADING IN THE CREEK.

THIS WATER IS TOO DARN COLD.
YOU COULD GO SIT IN THE SHADE THEN.

THIS SHADE IS TOO DARN DARK.
YOU COULD GO SIT IN YOUR ROOM WITH THE WINDOWS SHUT AND THE FAN AND LIGHTS ON.

THAT'S WHAT I WAS DOING WHEN MOM THREW ME OUT HERE.
I WAS KIDDING.

GIVE ME SOME COOKIES, OR I SOAK YOU WITH THIS WATER BALLOON!

WHY, YOU LITTLE THUG! DON'T YOU THREATEN YOUR MOTHER! AND DON'T EVEN **THINK** ABOUT THROWING THAT IN THE HOUSE!

OUT! OUT!

I'LL BET I'D HAVE GOTTEN SOME COOKIES IF I HAD FILLED THIS WITH **PAINT**.

Calvin and HOBBES

by WATTERSON

Z

IT'S JULY ALREADY! OH NO! OH NO!

I'LL SAY! MY BOOK SAYS THAT THIS ONE WASP LAYS ITS EGG ON A SPIDER, SO WHEN THE EGG HATCHES, THE LARVA EATS THE SPIDER, SAVING THE VITAL ORGANS FOR LAST, SO THE SPIDER STAYS ALIVE WHILE IT'S BEING DEVOURED!

Calvin and Hobbes
by WATTERSON

DO RE MI FA SO LA TI DO

A SPARROW ALIGHTS UPON A TREE BRANCH.

BUT THIS IS NO ORDINARY SPARROW! THIS IS A SONG SPARROW!

SWAYING GENTLY IN THE BREEZE, HE PREPARES TO BURST FORTH IN RAPTUROUS MELODY!

ON TOP OF SPA-GHETTI

ALL COVERED WITH CHEEEESE, I LOST MY POOR MEEEATBALLL, WHEN...

WATTERSON

DAD, HOW DOES A LIGHT BULB WORK?
MAGIC.

DIDN'T YOU SAY THAT'S HOW THE VACUUM CLEANER WORKS?
RIGHT. THEY'RE BOTH MAGIC.

YOU JUST DON'T KNOW HOW THEY WORK, I'LL BET.
FINE. DON'T BELIEVE YOUR OWN FATHER, WHO'S BEEN AROUND A LOT LONGER THAN YOU.

LOOK MOM, MAGIC!
THAT'S NOT MAGIC!

WHEN YOU WISH UPON A STAR YOUR DREAMS COME TRUE.

I WISH I HAD A COOL MILLION DOLLARS RIGHT NOW!

IF JIMINY CRICKET WAS HERE, I'D SKOOSH HIM.

WHAP

I DID IT! I CAUGHT IT!

I'M OUT,

Calvin and Hobbes
by WATTERSON

WATTERSON

YOU'RE OUT!
DOINK!

I THINK THE BASES ARE TOO DARN FAR APART.
AHH, YOU'RE JUST A BIG SISSY.

FINE, I WILL. AND **YOU** CAN START WASHING YOUR **OWN** CLOTHES, AND FIXING YOUR **OWN** MEALS, AND PICKING UP YOUR **OWN** TOYS, AND MAKING YOUR **OWN** BED, AND CLEANING UP YOUR **OWN** MESSES, DAY AFTER DAY AFTER **DAY**!

Calvin and Hobbes

by WATTERSON

WHAT ARE YOU WRITING?
I'M TELLING THESE COMPANIES I INTEND TO BOYCOTT ALL THEIR PRODUCTS IF THEY DON'T PULL THEIR ADS FROM A TV SHOW I FIND OFFENSIVE.

BY GOLLY, IF THESE COMPANIES ARE GOING TO SUPPORT OBJECTIONABLE TV PROGRAMS, I'LL TAKE MY BUSINESS ELSEWHERE!

MAYBE I CAN SCARE AWAY THE ADVERTISING DOLLARS AND GET THE SHOW CANCELED.

WHY DON'T YOU JUST NOT WATCH THE SHOW?
THIS CLEAN, WHOLESOME TELEVISION! UGHH, IT MAKES ME SICK.

I NEVER LIKED ICE CREAM CONES TOO MUCH UNTIL I DISCOVERED A NEW WAY TO EAT THEM.

I BITE OFF THE BOTTOM OF THE CONE AND SUCK OUT THE ICE CREAM AS IT GETS SOFT.

YOU WOULDN'T BELIEVE SOME OF THE AWFUL NOISES YOU CAN MAKE, AND IT GETS PRETTY SLOPPY WHEN THE CONE GETS SOGGY AND BOTH ENDS START DRIPPING.

IN MY BOOK, FOOD SHOULD BE NUTRITION AND ENTERTAINMENT.
THAT'S WHY WE TIGERS LIKE OUR FOOD SURPRISED AND RUNNING.

I'M SO SMART IT'S ALMOST SCARY. I GUESS I'M A CHILD PROGENY.

MOST CHILDREN ARE.

HUH?
NOTHING.

PEOPLE THINK IT MUST BE FUN TO BE A SUPER GENIUS, BUT THEY DON'T REALIZE HOW HARD IT IS TO PUT UP WITH ALL THE IDIOTS IN THE WORLD.
ISN'T YOUR PANTS ZIPPER SUPPOSED TO BE IN THE FRONT?

Calvin and HOBBES
by WATTERSON
DARLINGGG, I'M HOME! ..AND I BROUGHT A SURPRISE!

LET'S HOPE IT'S A DIVORCE!

DARLING, I STOPPED AT THE HOSPITAL ON THE WAY HOME FROM WORK.
DON'T CALL ME "DARLING," OK?

I BROUGHT HOME OUR NEW BABY!
A BABY?! I DON'T WANT A BABY!

WHAT SHALL WE NAME HIM?
OUR BABY IS A RABBIT?!? HOW COME WE HAVE A RABBIT?!

HE'S NOT A RABBIT, HE'S A LITTLE BOY! WE'LL CALL HIM "JEFFREY," OK?
HE LOOKS LIKE A RABBIT TO ME.

WELL, JUST PRETEND HE'S A BABY!
NO! THIS IS IDIOTIC! I REFUSE!!

PLAYING "HOUSE" MAKES ME SICK! I'M LEAVING!
I DON'T SEE WHY YOU'LL PLAY PRETEND WITH YOUR DUMB OL' TIGER, BUT NOT WITH MR. BUN!
WATTERSON

WELL, THERE'S NO DELAYING THE INEVITABLE. LET'S GET IN THE CAR.

WHERE ARE WE GOING?
THE SAME PLACE WE GO **EVERY** SUMMER: CAMPING ON SOME DESOLATE ROCK AT THE END OF THE EARTH.

AGAIN?
YEP. THIS IS HOW DAD LIKES TO UNWIND.

WITH EVERYONE COMPLAINING?
RIGHT. HE LIKES TO WATCH US ALL SUFFER.

LOOK, DAD, THERE'S A TOWN COMING UP. SEE THE SIGN?
ton

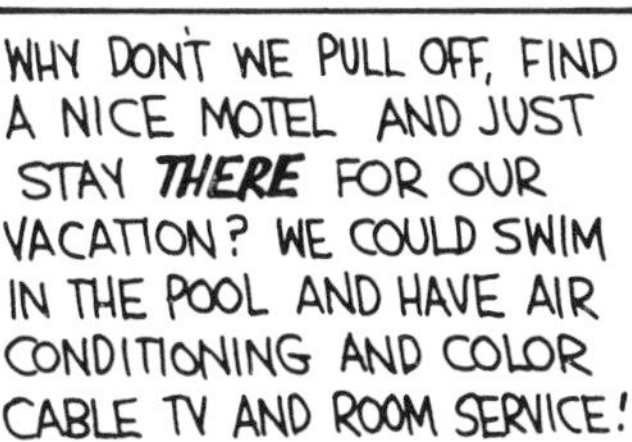
WHY DON'T WE PULL OFF, FIND A NICE MOTEL AND JUST STAY **THERE** FOR OUR VACATION? WE COULD SWIM IN THE POOL AND HAVE AIR CONDITIONING AND COLOR CABLE TV AND ROOM SERVICE!

NO ONE WOULD HAVE TO KNOW WE DIDN'T CAMP! **I** WOULDN'T TELL ANYONE! WE COULD EVEN GO TO THE STORE, BUY A BIG FISH, TAKE YOUR PICTURE WITH IT, AND SAY YOU CAUGHT IT! CAN'T WE, DAD? CAN'T WE TURN OFF HERE?

YES, LET'S!
NOW DON'T **YOU** START!

TA DA! WE'RE HERE!
GOOD OL' "ITCHY ISLAND," HOME OF THE NUCLEAR MOSQUITOES.

BUG BITES BUILD CHARACTER.
YEAH, AND LAST YEAR YOU SAID DIARRHEA BUILDS CHARACTER.

SO THINK WHAT A FINE YOUNG MAN YOU'RE GROWING UP TO BE.
...IF ALL THIS CHARACTER DOESN'T KILL ME FIRST.

THAT REMINDS ME, OPEN THE DUFFEL BAG AND GET OUT THE SPAM.
IF THE CANOE ISN'T HERE IN THE MORNING, IT MEANS HOBBES AND I STRUCK OUT FOR HOME.

BOY, IT'S GREAT TO BE HERE! THIS IS THE LIFE! I THINK I'LL JUMP IN FOR A SWIM. WANT TO JOIN ME?
NO, THANKS.

AW, C'MON. IT'LL FEEL GREAT.
RIGHT. THAT LAKE COULDN'T HAVE MELTED BEFORE YESTERDAY.

HEY, LET'S GO FOR A SWIM!
SURE, DAD. I'D LOVE TO START THE WEEK WITH A LITTLE HYPOTHERMIA.

I THINK WHAT I LIKE BEST ABOUT VACATIONS IS THE FAMILY TOGETHERNESS.

WAKE UP, CALVIN. IT'S 5:30 AND YOU CAN SEE THE FISH JUMPING.
MMF. GOWAY.

IT'S A BEAUTIFUL MORNING. THE SUN'S BARELY UP AND THERE'S A MIST OVER THE WATER. IT'S PERFECTLY STILL. NOT A SOUL ANYWHERE! DON'T YOU WANT TO SEE THIS?
LEEMEE LONE.

I THOUGHT YOU SAID YOU WANTED TO GO FISHING. YOU'VE GOT TO GET UP EARLY IF YOU WANT TO CATCH ANYTHING. C'MON, THE CANOE'S ALL READY AND I'VE GOT YOUR FISHING ROD.
MOM, MAKE DAD GO AWAY!

ANOTHER THING I LIKE ABOUT VACATIONS IS THE SHARING OF SPECIAL MOMENTS.

WELL, I GUESS THAT'S ENOUGH FISHING FOR NOW. MMM, I CAN'T WAIT TO GET BACK AND HAVE BREAKFAST! I CAN ALMOST SMELL THE COFFEE FROM HERE! WHAT A LIFE!

HEY, WHERE IS EVERY...

THERE'S GOING TO BE A SMALLMOUTH BASS FLOPPING IN SOME SLEEPING BAGS IN A MINUTE OR TWO!

YOU KNOW, I REALLY LIKE IT WHEN YOU GO OFF TO WORK IN THE MORNINGS.
IT'S 6:30 ALREADY! ARE YOU PEOPLE GOING TO WASTE THE WHOLE DAY?

I'LL BET I'M MISSING SOME GREAT TV SHOWS.

WHATCHA DOIN', DAD? PAINTING A PICTURE?
YEP.

YOU'RE GIVING YOUR HARMONICA SKILLS A REAL RUN FOR THE MONEY.
WHO ASKED YOU?

SNIFF SNIFF
Z
HEY, WHAT ARE YOU DOING? ARE YOU AWAKE?

SNIFF SNIFF SMACK SMACK
YOU'RE DREAMING, STUPID. WAKE UP.

MM! WHY YES, THANK YOU, SOME GOOD FRESH FISH WOULD HIT THE SPOT! OOH, THERE'S A NICE BIG ONE!
AAUGH!

I DON'T CARE **WHAT** ALL YOUR CLOTHES SMELL LIKE! I'M NOT WASHING ANYTHING NOW! GO TO BED!

MAN, I CAN'T WAIT TO GET IN THE CAR AND CRANK UP THE A/C AND SOME TUNES. SHAKE A LEG, HUH?

WATERSON

Calvin and HOBBES
by WATTERSON
FWOOSH

HEH HEH HEH...
BALLOONS

YOU'RE IN TROUBLE NOW, HOBBES! HEH HEH HEH!

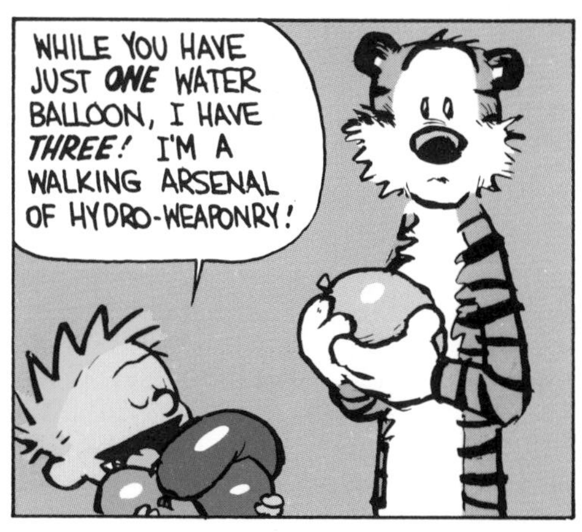
WHILE YOU HAVE JUST ONE WATER BALLOON, I HAVE THREE! I'M A WALKING ARSENAL OF HYDRO-WEAPONRY!

HA HA! I CAN SEE THE FEAR IN YOUR EYES! YOU REALIZE THAT I CAN GET YOU THREE TIMES WETTER THAN YOU CAN GET ME!

THROW YOUR BALLOON, AND YOUR UTTER SOGGINESS IS ASSURED! I, ON THE OTHER HAND, CAN ACT WITH IMPUNITY! WITH THREE BALLOONS, I FEAR NOTHING!

CATCH.
HEY! DON'T! MY ARMS ARE FULL!

OH NO!

SPLOOSH
GISSHH
SPLASH
FWOOSH

WE SUPER-POWERS HAVE IT TOUGH.
MAYBE YOU SHOULD STOCK UP ON BRAINS INSTEAD!

OFF TO WORK, EH, DAD?
YEP.

IT SURE IS A NICE DAY. THE KIND OF DAY JUST MADE FOR SITTING UNDER A TREE AND READING A GOOD NOVEL COVER TO COVER, DON'T YOU THINK?

TOO BAD THAT'S A LUXURY AT YOUR AGE. WELL, MAYBE YOU CAN DO IT WHEN YOU'RE 65. I'M SURE YOU'LL BE THAT OLD BEFORE YOU KNOW IT. ENJOY YOUR DAY AT WORK.

DAD SURE IS SURLY IN THE MORNINGS.

YOU KNOW WHAT'S WEIRD? I DON'T REMEMBER MUCH OF ANYTHING UNTIL I WAS THREE YEARS OLD.

HALF OF MY LIFE IS A COMPLETE BLANK! I MUST'VE BEEN BRAINWASHED!

GOOD HEAVENS, WHAT KIND OF SICKO WOULD BRAINWASH AN INFANT?! AND WHAT DID I KNOW THAT SOMEONE WANTED ME TO FORGET??

BOY, AM I MYSTERIOUS.
I SEEM TO RECALL YOU SPENT MOST OF THE TIME BURPING UP.

MOM! THERE'S A BIG HORSEFLY ON THE BACK OF YOUR HEAD! DON'T MOVE! I'LL GET IT!

IS IT STILL THERE? YOU DIDN'T MOVE, DID YOU?
GET AWAY FROM ME!

Calvin and Hobbes
by WATTERSON
AHH... A DAY AT THE LAKE! THIS WILL BE GREAT!

I STILL DON'T SEE WHY WE CAN'T JUST SIT IN THE CAR WITH THE AIR CONDITIONER ON.

I'M GETTING SAND IN MY SUIT! I DON'T WANT TO SIT ON THE BEACH!

THIS WATER'S TOO COLD! I'M FREEZING TO DEATH!

OUT HERE THERE'S TOO MUCH SUN! I'LL GET SUNBURNED!

THIS LOTION MAKES ME GREASY AND MY SHIRT MAKES ME TOO HOT!

I DON'T WANT TO SIT IN THE SHADE! THIS IS BORING!

I HATE WALKING! MY LEGS ARE TIRED AND THE SAND IS TOO HOT AND THE WATER IS TOO COLD AND THERE'S NO SHADE HERE AND I'VE STILL GOT SAND IN MY SUIT!
WATTERSON

WHAT? ARE WE GOING ALREADY?

ARR! WE'RE BLOODTHIRSTY PIRATES!

AVAST, YE SCURVY DOGS! HOIST THE JOLLY ROGER AND READY THE PLANK!

HERE.
WHAT'S THIS?

OUR BOOTY!

HEY, MOM, DID YOU KNOW THAT GRAVITY IN OUTER SPACE WORKS AS IF SPACE WAS A SOFT, FLAT SURFACE? IT'S TRUE.

HEAVY MATTER, LIKE PLANETS, SINKS INTO THE SURFACE AND ANYTHING PASSING BY, LIKE LIGHT, WILL "ROLL" TOWARD THE DIP IN SPACE MADE BY THE PLANET. LIGHT IS ACTUALLY DEFLECTED BY GRAVITY! AMAZING, HUH?

AND SPEAKING OF GRAVITY, I DROPPED A PITCHER OF LEMONADE ON THE KITCHEN FLOOR WHEN MY ROLLER SKATES SLIPPED.

HOW CAN KIDS KNOW SO MUCH AND STILL BE SO DUMB?

YOU KNOW, THE WORLD SHOULD'VE BEEN DESIGNED SO EVERYONE DIDN'T HAVE TO EAT EACH OTHER TO SURVIVE. THERE SHOULD JUST BE FEWER PEOPLE AND ANIMALS TO BEGIN WITH.

AND THE WORLD CERTAINLY COULD'VE USED A MORE EVEN DISTRIBUTION OF ITS RESOURCES, THAT'S FOR SURE.

I WONDER WHY NOBODY CONSULTED YOU.
INCREDIBLE, ISN'T IT?

Calvin and HOBBES
by WATTERSON

WHY DOES THE SKY TURN RED AS THE SUN SETS?
THAT'S ALL THE OXYGEN IN THE ATMOSPHERE CATCHING FIRE.

WHERE DOES THE SUN GO WHEN IT SETS?
THE SUN SETS IN THE WEST. IN ARIZONA ACTUALLY, NEAR FLAGSTAFF.

OH.
THAT'S WHY THE ROCKS THERE ARE SO RED.

DON'T THE PEOPLE GET BURNED UP?
NO, THE SUN GOES OUT AS IT SETS. THAT'S WHY IT'S DARK AT NIGHT.

DOESN'T THE SUN CRUSH THE WHOLE STATE WHEN IT LANDS?
HA HA, OF COURSE NOT. HOLD A QUARTER UP. SEE, THE SUN'S JUST ABOUT THE SAME SIZE.

I THOUGHT I READ THAT THE SUN WAS REALLY BIG.
YOU CAN'T BELIEVE EVERYTHING YOU READ, I'M AFRAID.

SO HOW DOES THE SUN RISE IN THE EAST IF IT LANDS IN ARIZONA EACH NIGHT?
WELL, TIME FOR BED.
WATTERSON

I HOPE SOMEDAY I'M AS SMART AS DAD IS.
WHY, WHAT DID HE TELL YOU NOW?

I PERFORMED A SCIENTIFIC EXPERIMENT TODAY.
WATTERSON

YOU KNOW HOW MAPS ALWAYS SHOW NORTH AS UP AND SOUTH AS DOWN? I WANTED TO SEE IF THAT WAS TRUE OR NOT.

WHAT DID YOU FIND OUT?
NOT MUCH. YOUR COMPASS DIDN'T SURVIVE THE TRIP SOUTH FROM THE TOP OF THE TREE.

MY COMPASS?!
LET ME KNOW WHEN YOU GET A NEW ONE. MY JUNIOR SCIENTIST BOOK SAYS NOT TO GET DISCOURAGED BY TEMPORARY SETBACKS.

I'VE BEEN THINKING. YOU KNOW HOW BORING DAD IS? MAYBE IT'S A BIG PHONY ACT!

MAYBE AFTER HE PUTS US TO BED, DAD DONS SOME WEIRD COSTUME AND GOES OUT FIGHTING CRIME! MAYBE THIS WHOLE "DAD" STUFF IS JUST A SECRET IDENTITY!

MAYBE THE MAYOR CALLS DAD ON A SECRET HOT LINE WHENEVER THE CITY'S IN TROUBLE! MAYBE DAD'S A MASKED SUPERHERO!
WATTERSON

IF THAT'S TRUE HE SHOULD DRIVE A COOLER CAR.
I KNOW. OURS DOESN'T EVEN HAVE A CASSETTE DECK.

THERE'S THE STEGOSAURUS OUT FRONT! THERE'S THE NATURAL HISTORY MUSEUM! HOORAY!

I CAN'T WAIT TO SEE ALL THE DINOSAURS! C'MON, LET'S HURRY!
WATTERSON

IT'S CERTAINLY BEEN A WHILE SINCE WE'VE BEEN HERE, HASN'T IT?

AT THE MUSEUM'S REQUEST, YES.
OH, THAT'S RIGHT. CALVIN, NO BITING PEOPLE THIS TIME, REMEMBER?
RROWRR

WHAT KIND OF DINOSAUR DID YOU SAY THIS WAS?
IT'S A STEGOSAURUS!

HE LOOKS PRETTY FEROCIOUS.
NO, HE WAS A PLANT EATER. THE TAIL SPIKES WERE FOR SELF-DEFENSE.

OH. DID TYRANNOSAURS FIGHT THESE?
OF COURSE NOT, MOM! TYRANNOSAURS CAME MILLIONS OF YEARS LATER!

LOOK, TRY NOT TO EMBARRASS ME WHEN WE GO INSIDE, OK?
WHY ARE WE GOING HERE IF HE ALREADY KNOWS EVERYTHING?

LOOK, HOBBES, HERE'S AN ANCESTOR OF YOURS! A SABER-TOOTHED TIGER!

HA HA, I'LL BET HE WAS POPULAR! IF ANYONE NEEDED TO OPEN A CAN OF JUICE, THEY'D JUST PUT HIM OVER IT AND HIT HIM ON THE HEAD! HA HA!

HEE HEE, I'LL BET THEY DIED OUT BECAUSE THEY COULDN'T UNDERSTAND EACH OTHER! THEY PWOBABBY DOKKED WIKE DIFF! HA HA HA!

... ALL IN ALL, THOUGH, THEY WERE UNDOUBTEDLY THE PINNACLE OF PREHISTORIC EVOLUTION..

LOOK, MOM, THE MUSEUM HAS A GIFT SHOP!

CAN I BUY SOMETHING? THEY'VE GOT DINOSAUR BOOKS, DINOSAUR MODELS, DINOSAUR T-SHIRTS, DINOSAUR POSTERS..

I DON'T THINK YOU NEED ANY MORE DINOSAUR STUFF, CALVIN.
BUT MOM, IT'S ALL EDUCATIONAL! YOU WANT ME TO LEARN, DON'T YOU??

BOY, SHE FELL FOR THAT ONE.
I'LL SAY! I WONDER IF WE COULD GET ANY BATMAN JUNK THIS WAY.

Calvin and HOBBES
by WATTERSON

WATTERSON

OH NO, YOU DON'T! THERE'S ONLY ROOM FOR ONE IN THIS POOL AND I WAS HERE FIRST!

IF **YOU** WANT TO COOL OFF, YOU'LL JUST HAVE TO JUMP IN THE SPRINKLER.
FINE! I'LL **DO** THAT.

!

DOGGONE IT, I DIDN'T MEAN FOR YOU TO HAVE **FUN**!

Z
Z

CRAACKK

BOOM

WHAT DO YOU THINK? A THUNDERSTORM, OR A SPACE ALIEN RAY GUN INVASION?
WHICHEVER, TELL ME WHEN IT'S OVER.

HOW'S IT COMING?
SLOW. THIS DIRT IS REALLY HARD.

WELL, THAT'S A PRETTY GOOD START.
BUT I'VE BEEN DIGGING ALL MORNING! THIS IS GOING TO TAKE FOREVER!

MAYBE YOU'LL HAVE TO SETTLE FOR A SMALLER SWIMMING POOL.
YEAH. THIS WOULD KILL YOU IF YOU WENT OFF THE HIGH DIVE.

IT'S TOO BAD. MOM WOULD'VE REALLY BEEN SURPRISED TO HAVE AN OLYMPIC POOL WHERE HER GARDEN USED TO BE.
MAYBE SHE'LL BE SURPRISED ANYWAY.

Calvin and Hobbes by WATTERSON

THERE! A FULL PITCHER OF "CALVIN'S CURATIVE ELIXIR"! WE'LL CHARGE PEOPLE A BUCK A GLASS AND GET RICH!

BUT THAT'S JUST DIRTY WATER FROM THE DRAINAGE DITCH! THERE ARE LEAVES IN IT!
"FORTIFIED WITH CHLOROPHYLL," WE'LL SAY.

NOBODY'S GOING TO PAY TO DRINK THAT! ANYONE CAN SEE IT'S FILTHY! IT'S SLUDGE!
HMM... MAYBE YOU'RE RIGHT.

PITCHER OF PLAGUE
Calvin's DEBILitating DISEASE DRINK!
$1.00 Not to have any
WATERSON

I'VE DECIDED NOT TO GO TO SCHOOL THIS FALL.

I DON'T NEED AN EDUCATION. I DON'T NEED TO LEARN THINGS. I DON'T NEED TO DEVELOP SKILLS. IT'S TOO MUCH TROUBLE.

HOW ARE YOU GOING TO MAKE IT IN THE WORLD IF YOU DON'T KNOW ANYTHING AND YOU DON'T HAVE ANY SKILLS?!

I'LL GO ON TALK SHOWS AND HYPE MYSELF.
WATERSON

UGHH, THERE ARE TIMES WHEN I HATE OWNING A HOUSE. ALL THE MAINTENANCE!
WATERSON

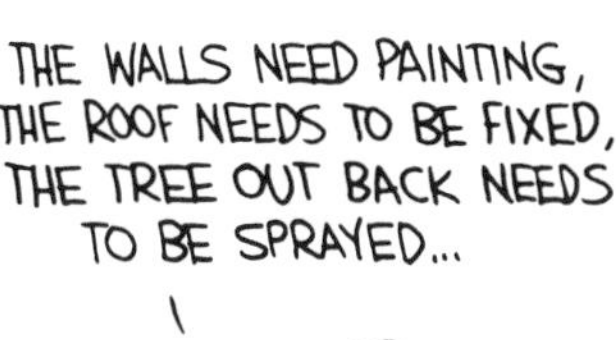
THE WALLS NEED PAINTING, THE ROOF NEEDS TO BE FIXED, THE TREE OUT BACK NEEDS TO BE SPRAYED...

IT SEEMS LIKE THE WHOLE PLACE IS FALLING APART.

...AND WHAT ISN'T FALLING APART IS BEING ACTIVELY DESTROYED!

Calvin and HOBBES
by WATTERSON
A 30-TON BRONTOSAURUS

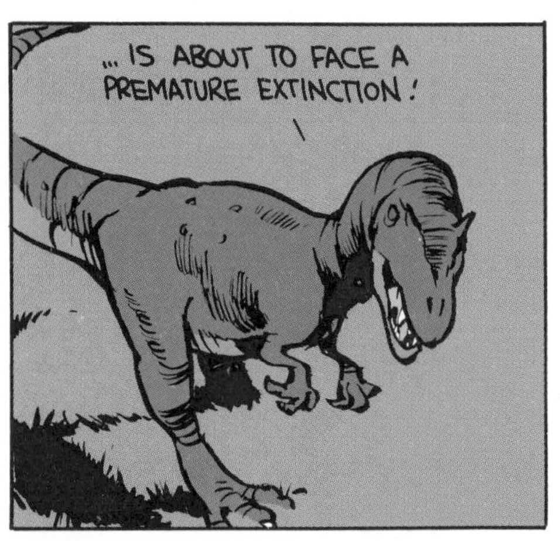
... IS ABOUT TO FACE A PREMATURE EXTINCTION!

THE ALLOSAURUS, FEARSOME PREDATOR OF THE JURASSIC, STALKS HIS PREY!

THE HERD OF BRONTOSAURS IS UNAWARE OF HIS PRESENCE!

SPOTTING A STRAGGLER, THE ALLOSAURUS LUNGES!

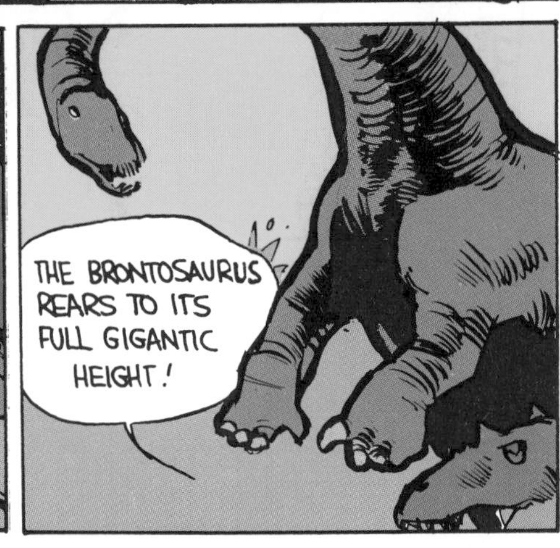
THE BRONTOSAURUS REARS TO ITS FULL GIGANTIC HEIGHT!

WHAT INDUCES AN ALLOSAURUS TO ATTACK A MONSTER MORE THAN TWICE HIS OWN SIZE??

I'M HUNGRY!
THE HAMBURGERS ARE COOKING! NOW GET OFF ME!
WATTERSON

CALVIN THE HUMMINGBIRD ZIPS BY WITH A LOUD WHIR!

ALTHOUGH SMALL, HE PUTS OUT TREMENDOUS ENERGY. TO HOVER, HIS WINGS BEAT HUNDREDS OF TIMES EACH SECOND!

WHAT FUELS THIS INCREDIBLE METABOLISM? CONCENTRATED SUGAR WATER! HE DRINKS HALF HIS WEIGHT A DAY!

...PREFERABLY LOADED WITH CAFFEINE.
ARE YOU DRINKING MORE SODA POP?!
SLURRPP

"ONCE UPON A TIME THERE WAS..."
HOLD IT.

WHAT'S THE MATTER?
HAS THIS BOOK BEEN A BEST SELLER? HAS THE AUTHOR WON A PULITZER? DID THE NEW YORK TIMES LIKE IT?

I ONLY WANT STORIES THAT COME HIGHLY RECOMMENDED. ARE THERE ANY LAUDATORY QUOTES ON THE DUST JACKET?

AHEM... "ONCE UPON A TIME THERE WAS A NOISY KID WHO STARTED GOING TO BED WITHOUT A STORY."
HAS THIS BOOK BEEN MADE INTO A MOVIE? COULD WE BE WATCHING THIS ON VIDEO?

WHAT ARE YOU DOING?
I'M PRACTICING MY SNEERS.

THERE'S NOTHING LIKE A GOOD SNEER TO DRY UP CONVERSATION. HOW'S MINE LOOK?

AWFUL!
THANKS. WITH THIS SNEER, I HOPE TO BE AN UNBEARABLE BURDEN AT ANY SOCIAL OCCASION.

THAT WILL GIVE YOU A REAL HEAD START ON BEING A TEEN-AGER.
I KNOW! IT'S LIKE GETTING SEVEN EXTRA YEARS!

Calvin and HOBBES
by WATTERSON

HEADS UP!
GISHHH

YOU ROTTEN FLEABAG! I'LL GET YOU! YOU HEAR ME?! SAY YOUR PRAYERS!
AHH, YOU'RE ALL WET! HEE HEE!

BY GOLLY, I'LL SOAK HIM WITH THE HOSE! HE WON'T DRY OUT FOR A MONTH!

I'VE GOT YOU NOW, HOBBES, OL' "BUDDY"! HEH HEH HEH!

TRYING TO GET ANOTHER BALLOON READY, EH? WELL YOU'RE TOO LATE! HOPE YOU'RE THIRSTY, SUCKER!

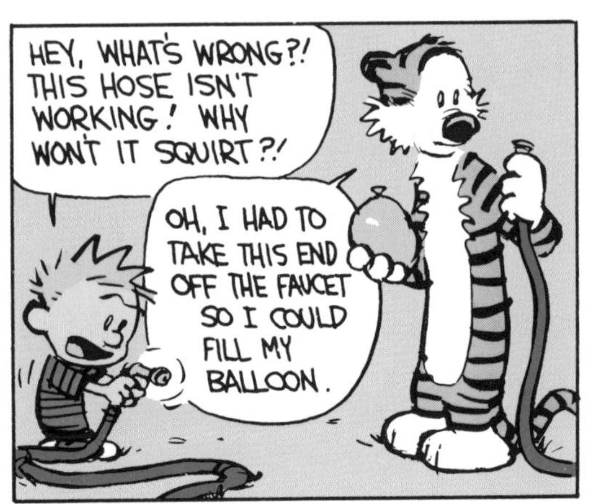
HEY, WHAT'S WRONG?! THIS HOSE ISN'T WORKING! WHY WON'T IT SQUIRT?!
OH, I HAD TO TAKE THIS END OFF THE FAUCET SO I COULD FILL MY BALLOON.

UH-OH.
WATTERSON

ACTUALLY, I'M KIND OF LOOKING FORWARD TO GOING TO SCHOOL NEXT WEEK.

WHAP!

TOO LATE! I MADE ANOTHER HOME RUN.
(PANT PANT) I'M QUITTING IF WE DON'T STOP USING THIS TENNIS BALL.

AAAGH!!

YOU SHOULD BE MORE ALERT! YOU WOULDN'T LAST TWO SECONDS IN THE JUNGLE.
THAT'S WHY I LIVE *HERE*, YOU DOLT!

WHAT ARE YOU DOING DOWN THERE, CALVIN?
SHH, MOM! GO AWAY! SUSIE'S COMING DOWN THE WALK AND I'M GOING TO THROW SOME CRAB APPLES AT HER.

OH, NO, YOU'RE NOT! PUT THOSE DOWN!
AWWW, MOM!

DON'T THROW CRAB APPLES AT *ANY*ONE. THEY'RE HARD AND YOU COULD REALLY HURT SOMEONE.
OK, OK.

WHAT ARE YOU DOING DOWN THERE, CALVIN?
SHH, SUSIE! GO AWAY! I'M GOING TO THROW THIS SQUISHY OLD TOMATO AT MY MOM.

MOM WANTS ME TO MAKE MY BED. COME HELP ME, OK?
OK.

YOU GET SOME PENCILS, AND I'LL GET SOME BIG PAPER!
I THOUGHT WE WERE MAKING THE BED.

AND DO ALL THAT WORK?!? NO, WE'RE GOING TO INVENT A ROBOT TO MAKE THE BED FOR US!

WONT INVENTING A ROBOT BE MORE WORK THAN MAKING THE BED?
IT'S ONLY WORK IF SOMEBODY MAKES YOU DO IT.

HOW ARE WE GOING TO INVENT A ROBOT? WE DON'T KNOW ANYTHING ABOUT MACHINES.
MAYBE YOU DON'T.

IT'S EASY. THERE ARE JUST FOUR SIMPLE MACHINES TO ALTER FORCE: THE LEVER, THE PULLEY, THE INCLINED PLANE AND, UM, THE INTERNAL COMBUSTION ENGINE.

TAKE MY WORD FOR IT, I'M AN EXPERT AT INVENTIONS.
SO WHERE DO WE START?

WE ASK MOM FOR A RESEARCH GRANT.

HI, MOM. CAN I LOOK AT YOUR WALLET FOR A FEW MINUTES? I, UH, WANT TO SEE SOMETHING.
HOLD ON. DID YOU MAKE YOUR BED LIKE I ASKED YOU?

I'M WORKING ON IT.
AS I RECALL, YOUR BED IS IN YOUR ROOM.

I'M INVENTING A ROBOT TO MAKE THE BED, BUT I NEED A GRANT. CAN I HAVE $50?

WHAT'D SHE SAY? DID YOU GET THE MONEY?
BOY, WHEN WE'RE THE COVER STORY OF POPULAR MECHANICS, I'LL HAVE SOME CHOICE WORDS TO SAY ABOUT FAMILY ENCOURAGEMENT.

OK, THE FIRST THING OUR ROBOT NEEDS IS A HEAD.
SHOULD WE USE A COFFEE CAN?

NO, THAT'S TOO SMALL. THE HEAD HAS TO HOLD THIS TAPE RECORDER. SEE, I'VE MADE RECORDINGS FOR THE ROBOT'S VOICE!

REALLY?
SURE! THIS WAY, OUR ROBOT NOT ONLY COMMUNICATES, BUT WE CAN ALSO "PROGRAM" HIM TO HAVE THE PROPER PERSONALITY!

PERSONALITY?
RIGHT. ROBOTS SHOULD BE RESPECTFUL.
CLICK HOW MAY I EASE YOUR LIFE, OH GRAND EXALTED MASTER?
WATTERSON

HEY, DAD, I'M INVENTING A ROBOT. CAN YOU GET ME A PATENT?
YOU INVENTED A ROBOT?

WELL, HERE IT IS SO FAR. HOBBES AND I HAVE BEEN WORKING ON IT ALL AFTERNOON. IT'S NOT QUITE PERFECTED YET, BUT YOU GET THE IDEA.
WATTERSON

HMM... WHAT DOES IT DO?
THAT'S THE PROBLEM. WE HAVEN'T FIGURED OUT HOW TO MAKE IT DO WHAT WE WANT.

DON'T GET DISCOURAGED. YOUR MOM AND I GOT THE SAME RESULTS AFTER WORKING ON YOU FOR SIX YEARS.
HAR HAR. MY ATTORNEY IS A COMEDIAN.

WELL, HOBBES, WE MIGHT AS WELL GIVE UP. I CAN'T FIGURE OUT HOW TO MAKE A ROBOT. THIS ONE DOESN'T DO ANYTHING.

IT'S PAST YOUR BEDTIME, CALVIN. YOU'LL HAVE TO LEAVE YOUR TOYS FOR TOMORROW.
OK, MOM. OUR ROBOT WASN'T WORKING OUT ANYWAY.

GOSH, AND WE SPENT ALL DAY ON IT, TOO. I THOUGHT FOR SURE OUR ROBOT WOULD SAVE US FROM MAKING THE BED.

AND IN A WAY, HE DID!
HEY, YEAH! WE'RE GENIUSES!
WATTERSON

YOUR MOM SURE WAS CHEERFUL THIS MORNING.
HMPH.

I'VE NEVER SEEN HER HUMMING AND SASHAYING AROUND THE KITCHEN LIKE THAT.
HMPH.

HOW LONG HAVE WE BEEN WAITING FOR THE BUS NOW?

ABOUT TWO AND A HALF HOURS.
I THINK MOM PUT ME OUT HERE THIS EARLY ON PURPOSE.

HI, CALVIN! AREN'T YOU EXCITED ABOUT GOING TO SCHOOL? LOOK AT ALL THESE GREAT SCHOOL SUPPLIES I GOT! I LOVE HAVING NEW NOTEBOOKS AND STUFF!

ALL I'VE GOT TO SAY IS THEY'RE NOT MAKING ME LEARN ANY FOREIGN LANGUAGES! IF ENGLISH IS GOOD ENOUGH FOR ME, THEN BY GOLLY, IT'S GOOD ENOUGH FOR THE REST OF THE WORLD!

EVERYONE SHOULD SPEAK ENGLISH OR JUST SHUT UP, THAT'S WHAT I SAY!

YOU SHOULD MAYBE CHECK THE CHEMICAL CONTENT OF YOUR BREAKFAST CEREAL.
THEY CAN MAKE ME GO UNTIL GRADE EIGHT, AND THEN, FFFT, I'M OUTTA HERE!

CALVIN, WOULD YOU LEAD THE CLASS IN THE PLEDGE OF ALLEGIANCE?
NO!

WHAT DID THE SUPREME COURT DECIDE ABOUT THAT? IS THIS A PRAYER? DON'T YOU HAVE TO READ ME MY RIGHTS? I DON'T KEEP UP WITH THIS STUFF! I'M JUST A KID!

I'M ONLY HERE BECAUSE MY PARENTS MAKE ME GO! I DON'T WANT TO BE A TEST CASE! I DON'T EVEN KNOW WHAT COURT DISTRICT I'M IN! CALL ON SOMEONE ELSE!

CALVIN?
* SIGHHHH * I CAN'T BELIEVE IT'S NOT EVEN 8:15 YET.

THE FEARLESS SPACEMAN SPIFF IS BEING PURSUED ACROSS THE GALAXY BY DREADED SCUM BEINGS!

Calvin and Hobbes

by WATTERSON

UH OH, CALVIN THE REPTILE IS IN TROUBLE!
WATERSON

AS AN ECTOTHERM, HIS BODY RELIES ON THE ENVIRONMENT TO WARM OR COOL ITS TEMPERATURE.

NOW THAT IT'S COLDER OUTSIDE, CALVIN'S BODY TEMPERATURE FALLS AND HE BECOMES SLUGGISH! HE'LL GO INTO TORPOR IF HE CAN'T FIND A WARM PLACE TO LIE!

LEAVE THE THERMOSTAT ALONE, AND PUT ON A SWEATER IF YOU'RE COLD.
I..I DON'T HAVE THE EN..ENERGY!

I HEARD THAT BIG CATS DON'T PURR.
THAT'S TRUE. WE'RE TOO FIERCE AND FEROCIOUS. WE DON'T EVER PURR.
WELL WHAT DO YOU CALL THE NOISE YOU MAKE WHEN YOU GET YOUR TUMMY RUBBED?!
GROWLING FRIENDLY-LIKE.
WATERSON

CALVIN, YOUR MOM AND I LOOKED OVER YOUR REPORT CARD, AND WE THINK YOU COULD BE DOING BETTER.
BUT I DON'T LIKE SCHOOL.

WHY NOT? YOU LIKE TO READ AND YOU LIKE TO LEARN. I KNOW YOU DO.

I MEAN, YOU'VE READ EVERY DINOSAUR BOOK EVER WRITTEN, AND YOU'VE LEARNED A LOT, RIGHT? READING AND LEARNING ARE **FUN**.
YEAH..

SO WHY DON'T YOU LIKE SCHOOL?
WE DON'T READ ABOUT DINOSAURS.
WATERSON

Calvin and HOBBES
by WATTERSON

MMFF
I'VE DECIDED TO BE AN INTELLECTUAL.
WATTERSON

Calvin and Hobbes

by WATTERSON

DEAR, SOMETIME I WANT YOU TO LOOK AT THAT DISCOLORED SPOT ON THE RUG. IT SEEMS TO BE GETTING BIGGER ALL THE TIME.

MAY I LEAVE THE TABLE? LIKE RIGHT NOW?

I want that truck, Twinky.
IT'S MINE, MOE. I BROUGHT IT FROM HOME.

I said gimme the truck.
MOE, YOU CAN'T JUST **TAKE** THINGS FROM PEOPLE BECAUSE YOU'RE BIGGER!

I'm not taking it. You're **giving** it to me because we'll both be so much happier that way.

HOW TOUCHING.

MOE, GIVE ME MY TRUCK BACK. IT'S NOT YOURS.
It is **now**. You gave it to me.

I DIDN'T HAVE MUCH CHOICE, **DID** I ?! IT WAS EITHER GIVE UP THE TRUCK OR GET PUNCHED!
So?

SO I ONLY "GAVE" IT TO YOU BECAUSE YOU'RE BIGGER AND MEANER THAN ME!
Yeah? ...So?

THE FORENSIC MARVEL HAS REDUCED MY LOGIC TO SHAMBLES.
You're saying you changed your mind about getting punched?

THAT NO-GOOD, ROTTEN MOE! HE WON'T GIVE MY TRUCK BACK TO ME. THE OAF WILL PROBABLY BREAK IT, TOO.

SHOULD I STEAL IT BACK? I KNOW STEALING IS WRONG, BUT **HE** STOLE IT FROM **ME**, AND IF I **DON'T** STEAL IT BACK, MOE WILL JUST KEEP IT, AND THAT'S NOT FAIR.

THEY SAY TWO WRONGS DON'T MAKE A RIGHT, BUT WHAT ARE YOU SUPPOSED TO **DO** THEN? JUST LET THE BIGGEST GUY MAKE HIS OWN RULES ALL THE TIME? LET MIGHT MAKE RIGHT?

... THAT SOUNDS REASONABLE.

BY GOLLY, I **AM** GOING TO STEAL MY TRUCK BACK FROM MOE! IT'S MINE AND HE HAS NO RIGHT TO HAVE IT!

I'LL JUST SNEAK UP BEHIND THE SWINGS HERE, AND WHEN MOE'S NOT LOOKING, I'LL RUN UP, GRAB THE TRUCK AND TAKE OFF!

THIS PLAYGROUND SHOULD HAVE ONE OF THOSE AUTOMATIC INSURANCE MACHINES LIKE THEY HAVE IN AIRPORTS.

OK, MOE'S GOT HIS BACK TO ME! NOW I'LL ZIP OVER, STEAL MY TRUCK BACK AND RUN LIKE CRAZY!

HE'LL NEVER KNOW WHAT HIT HIM! BY THE TIME HE SEES THE TRUCK IS GONE, I'LL BE A MILE AWAY! IT'S A FAIL-PROOF PLAN! NOTHING CAN GO WRONG! IT'S A SNAP!

THERE'S NO REASON TO HESITATE. IT'LL BE OVER IN A SPLIT SECOND, AND I'LL SURE BE GLAD TO HAVE MY TRUCK BACK! I'LL JUST DO IT AND BE DONE! NOTHING TO IT! IT'S EASY!

OBVIOUSLY MY BODY DOESN'T BELIEVE A WORD MY BRAIN IS SAYING.

PHOOEY, WHO AM I KIDDING? I'D NEVER GET AWAY WITH STEALING MY TRUCK BACK FROM MOE. THE UGLY GALOOT IS THE SIZE OF A BUICK.

HMM... SINCE I CAN'T **FIGHT** HIM, MAYBE I SHOULD TRY **TALKING** TO HIM. MAYBE IF I REASONED WITH HIM, HE'D SEE **MY** SIDE.

MAYBE HE'D REALIZE THAT STEALING HURTS PEOPLE, AND MAYBE HE'D RETURN MY TRUCK **WILLINGLY**.

MAYBE IF I'M REALLY LUCKY I WON'T GO THROUGH LIFE WITH THE NICKNAME "OMELET FACE."

LISTEN, MOE, THAT'S MY TRUCK, AND I WANT IT BACK!
Yeah?

YEAH! IT'S MY FAVORITE TRUCK. YOU HAD NO RIGHT TO TAKE IT!
Yeah?

YEAH! SO GIVE IT BACK! NOW!
I'll fight you for it.

I'LL BET MY AUTOPSY REVEALS MY MOUTH IS TOO BIG.
C'mon, wimp!
WATTERSON

I'M NOT GOING TO FIGHT YOU, MOE! IF YOU WON'T GIVE ME MY TRUCK BACK, FINE! GO AHEAD AND KEEP IT!

YOU'RE THE ONE WHO HAS TO LIVE WITH YOURSELF! I CAN'T MAKE YOU DO WHAT'S RIGHT! YOU CAN HAVE THE STUPID TRUCK!

OK, thanks! Heh heh.

HEY, KID, IF YOU'RE NOT GONNA SWING, GET OFF AND LET SOMEONE ELSE ON, HUH?
WATTERSON

...SO MOE STOLE MY TRUCK, AND WHEN I TRIED TO GET IT BACK, MOE WANTED TO FIGHT ME FOR IT. I DIDN'T WANT TO FIGHT, SO I WALKED AWAY AND MOE KEPT MY TRUCK.

I DON'T UNDERSTAND IT, HOBBES. WHAT MAKES SOME PEOPLE SO GREEDY AND MEAN?

WHY IS IT THAT SOME PEOPLE DON'T CARE WHAT'S WRONG AND RIGHT? WHY DON'T PEOPLE TRY TO BE NICE TO EACH OTHER?

THE PROBLEM WITH PEOPLE IS THAT THEY'RE ONLY HUMAN.
WELL, YOU'RE LUCKY YOU DON'T HAVE TO BE ONE.
WATTERSON

YOU KNOW, SOMETIMES THE WORLD SEEMS LIKE A PRETTY MEAN PLACE.
THAT'S WHY ANIMALS ARE SO SOFT AND HUGGY.

...YEAH...

MOM! MOMM!

WHAT IS IT? WHAT'S THE MATTER?
HOBBES HAD A BAD DREAM.

YOU WOKE ME UP AT 2 A.M. BECAUSE YOU THINK YOUR STUFFED TIGER HAD A BAD DREAM?!?
HE DREAMED HE WAS SO HUNGRY, HE ATE US ALL UP.

I MUST BE HAVING A BAD DREAM.
DON'T YOU THINK YOU SHOULD MAKE HOBBES A SANDWICH, JUST IN CASE?

KNOW WHAT, DAD? AT THE FRESH FISH COUNTER IN THE SUPERMARKET, YOU CAN BUY REAL SQUID. THEY HAVE THEM IN A BUCKET.

THEY'RE REALLY GROSS.
MM, I'LL BET.

CALVIN, WHAT ARE YOU DOING?

Calvin and Hobbes
by WATTERSON
TIGERS ARE GREAT! THEY'RE THE TOAST OF THE TOWN. LIFE'S ALWAYS BETTER WHEN A TIGER'S AROUND!

CONSIDERING I OUTRANK YOU, I DON'T THINK I SHOULD HAVE TO DO THAT!

THIS MEETING OF THE TOP-SECRET CLUB G.R.O.S.S. (GET RID OF SLIMY GIRLS) WILL COME TO ORDER, SUPREME DICTATOR-FOR-LIFE CALVIN PRESIDING. ALL SALUTE!

OK, THE FIRST ORDER OF BUSINESS: PRESIDENT-AND-FIRST-TIGER HOBBES WILL READ THE MINUTES OF OUR LAST MEETING.

THANK YOU. 10:30 A.M.: READ MINUTES OF PREVIOUS MEETING. 10:31: DEBATED SO-CALLED "EDITORIAL SLANT" OF MINUTES. MUCH NONSENSE AND COMMOTION FROM DICTATOR-FOR-LIFE.
"NONSENSE"?!

10:32: PRESIDENT-AND-FIRST-TIGER OFFERS REASONABLE SOLUTION, BUT DICTATOR-FOR-LIFE TAKES NEEDLESS EXCEPTION.
REASONABLE SOLUTION?!? YOU TOLD ME TO GO JUMP IN A LAKE!

10:33: BLOWS EXCHANGED. DICTATOR-FOR-LIFE RECEIVES COMEUPPANCE.
HA! I BEAT YOU FAIR AND SQUARE! THESE MINUTES ARE NOTHING BUT LIES!

CALL ME A LIAR, WILL YOU?
BY GOLLY, I'LL CALL YOU WORSE THAN THAT!

CHOWDERHEAD!
MORON!
OGRE!
FLEABAG!

(PANT, PANT) TRUCE?
(GASP, PANT) OK, TRUCE.

WELL, ANOTHER PRODUCTIVE MEETING! WHAT A GREAT CLUB!
WATTERSON

HAVE YOU SEEN MY SHOES? I THOUGHT I HAD THEM OUT RIGHT HERE.

YOUR SHOES? I DON'T KNOW.
THEY **WERE** RIGHT HERE. WHERE COULD THEY HAVE GONE?

WE'RE GOING TO BE LATE.
WELL I CAN'T GO ANYWHERE WITHOUT MY **SHOES**. HELP ME LOOK.

THEY'RE NOT LEAVING **US** WITH A BABY SITTER TONIGHT!
WATTERSON

DING DONG
IT'S **ROSALYN**!
ANSWER THE DOOR, WILL YOU PLEASE, CALVIN?

HI ROZ. MY PARENTS CHANGED THEIR MINDS ABOUT GOING OUT, SO WE WON'T BE NEEDING YOUR SERVICES. GOODBYE.

HI, ROSALYN. WHAT ARE YOU TALKING ABOUT, CALVIN?
YOU CAN'T GO OUT IF MOM CAN'T FIND HER **SHOES**, RIGHT?

AND WHAT DO **YOU** KNOW ABOUT **THAT**?
I'D LIKE TO BE PAID IN ADVANCE TONIGHT.
UH, NOTHING! HA HA! UM, WHY? ARE HER SHOES MISSING?
WATTERSON

PHOOEY. MOM AND DAD LEFT. NOW WE'RE HERE ALONE WITH THE BABY SITTER FROM THE BLACK LAGOON.

HEE HEE! DO YOU THINK SHE REMEMBERS HOW LAST TIME WE THREATENED TO FLUSH HER SCIENCE NOTES DOWN THE TOILET?
HA HA HA! OUR FINEST MOMENT!

OK, YOU, GET IN BED.
WHAT?!
IT'S NOT EVEN 6:30!

SHE REMEMBERS, ALL RIGHT.
SHE CAN'T GET AWAY WITH THIS. WE'LL CALL THE RESCUE SQUAD.
WATTERSON

ROSALYN?
WHAT ARE YOU DOING OUT OF BED?

I THOUGHT I HEARD SOMETHING OUTSIDE.
I DIDN'T HEAR ANYTHING.

IT WAS KIND OF A THUMP. WILL YOU GO LOOK, AND MAKE SURE IT'S NOT ANY-THING SCARY?
I'LL CHECK, BUT I DIDN'T HEAR ANY THUMP.

YES...YES! GO OUT THE DOOR! TWO MORE STEPS! OH PLEASE, OH PLEASE! YES, YES, YES!
SEE? THERE'S NOTHING OUT HERE.

SEE, CALVIN? THERE'S NOTHING OUT HERE.
BUT I KNOW I HEARD SOMETHING! GO LOOK, OK? PLEASE?

OK, IF IT WILL MAKE YOU FEEL..
SLAM
HEY!

THIS WAS A TRICK?! WHY YOU SNEAKY LITTLE DRIP, I'LL GET YOU!!
HOBBES! I LOCKED HER OUT!

NOW WE CAN WATCH TV AND EAT COOKIES TILL WE'RE SICK! OH BOY!
THIS IS THE BEST WE'VE EVER BEEN BABY SAT!

CALVIN, YOU LET ME BACK IN THE HOUSE THIS INSTANT!

DON'T WORRY, ROSALYN! THERE'S ONLY A 50% CHANCE OF RAIN TONIGHT! HA HA!

SHE'S TRYING TO OPEN THE DOWNSTAIRS WINDOWS.
IT'S OK. I ALREADY LOCKED THEM.

YOU OPEN UP THAT DOOR!
HEY ROZ! WHAT'S IN YOUR PURSE? MIND IF WE LOOK??

CALVIN, I'M TELLING YOUR PARENTS ABOUT THIS! NOW LET ME IN!

PIPE DOWN, WILL YA ROZ? HOBBES AND I CAN HARDLY HEAR THE TV!

YOU'RE NOT SUPPOSED TO BE WATCHING TELEVISION!
HEY, IF YOU GO RENT US A VCR AND A MOVIE, WE'LL PUT THE TV NEAR A WINDOW SO YOU CAN WATCH TOO!

LET ME IN!
ARE YOU 18? YOU COULD GET US "VENUSIAN VAMPIRE VIXENS"!

CAL-VIN!
HANG ON, ROZ. THE PHONE IS RINGING!

I HOPE IT'S YOUR PARENTS! I HOPE THEY ASK TO TALK TO ME! BOY, YOU'LL BE IN TROUBLE THEN!

IT'S YOUR BOYFRIEND, CHARLIE! SHOULD I TELL HIM YOU'RE INDISPOSED? HA HA!

NO! LET ME TALK TO HIM!
SAY CHAS, DON'T YOU THINK YOU'RE SETTLING FOR TOO LITTLE IN THE GIRLFRIEND DEPARTMENT?

ISN'T IT GREAT TO GET OUT OF THE HOUSE ALONE TOGETHER FOR A CHANGE?
IT'S SO NICE AND QUIET. WE SHOULD DO THIS MORE OFTEN.

CALVIN, YOU'VE GOT FIVE SECONDS TO OPEN THE DOOR BEFORE I BREAK A WINDOW!
I'M TELLING YOU CHUCK, YOUR GIRLFRIEND IS A PSYCHO! I HOPE YOU'RE NOT MAKING ANY LONG-RANGE PLANS AROUND HER.

CALVIN, LISTEN CLOSELY. LOCKING ROSALYN OUT OF THE HOUSE WASN'T JUST **MEAN**, IT WAS **DANGEROUS**. IF YOU'D HURT YOURSELF OR IF THERE WAS A FIRE, SHE WOULDN'T HAVE BEEN ABLE TO HELP YOU.

Calvin and HOBBES
by WATTERSON
GISZH! ... GISZH!...

..GISZH!

OH, NO! IT'S THE MIDDLE OF RECESS AND THERE'S A TYRANNOSAURUS ON THE PLAYGROUND!

THE KIDS AT THE TOP OF THE SLIDE ARE THE FIRST TO GO! HOW IRONIC THAT THEY HAD PUSHED AND FOUGHT EACH OTHER TO BE THERE!

PANDEMONIUM ENSUES! TEACHERS LINE THE KIDS UP TO GO INSIDE, BUT THAT PROVES TO BE A SAD MISTAKE!

WALKING QUIETLY IN SINGLE FILE, THE KIDS ARE GOBBLED UP LIKE CHILDREN McNUGGETS!

SOON THE PLAYGROUND IS EMPTY! IT'S ALL HIS! THE TYRANNOSAUR LETS OUT A TRIUMPHANT ROAR!
WATTERSON

SAY, WHERE'S CALVIN? RECESS IS OVER. DIDN'T HE SEE US LINE UP TO COME IN?
I SEE HIM, MISS WORMWOOD! HE'S OUT BY THE SWINGS AND HE'S YELLING OR SOMETHING!

Calvin and Hobbes
by WATTERSON
THAT BIG, DUMB BULLY MOE PUNCHED ME AT SCHOOL YESTERDAY.
REALLY? WHAT DID YOU DO?

WELL, FIRST I SKIDDED ACROSS THE PLAYGROUND. THEN I CAROMED OFF A ROCK AND...

I WISH I HAD MORE FRIENDS, BUT PEOPLE ARE SUCH JERKS.

IF YOU CAN JUST GET MOST PEOPLE TO IGNORE YOU AND LEAVE YOU ALONE, YOU'RE DOING GOOD.

IF YOU CAN FIND EVEN ONE PERSON YOU REALLY LIKE, YOU'RE LUCKY.

...AND IF THAT PERSON CAN ALSO STAND YOU, YOU'RE REALLY LUCKY.

WHAT IF YOU FIND SOMEONE YOU CAN TALK TO WHILE YOU EAT APPLES ON A BRIGHT FALL MORNING?

WELL, YEAH... I SUPPOSE THERE'S NO POINT IN GETTING GREEDY, IS THERE?
WATTERSON

MAN, THIS IS BORING!

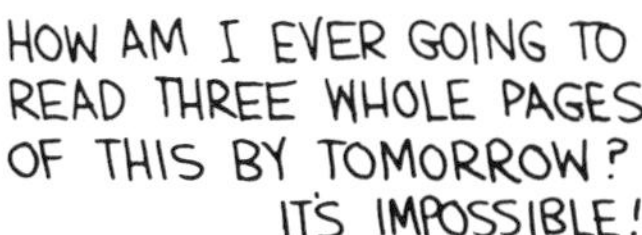
HOW AM I EVER GOING TO READ THREE WHOLE PAGES OF THIS BY TOMORROW?
IT'S IMPOSSIBLE!

... IMPOSSIBLE?? WHY, NOTHING'S IMPOSSIBLE!

NOT FOR... STUPENDOUS MAN!
BUM BA BA DAA DUM
BUM BA BA DAA DUM..

YES! IT'S... STUPENDOUS MAN! FRIEND OF FREEDOM! OPPONENT OF OPPRESSION! LOVER OF LIBERTY!

GREAT MOONS OF JUPITER! CALVIN (STUPENDOUS MAN'S 6-YEAR-OLD ALTER EGO) HAS THREE PAGES OF BORING HOMEWORK TO READ! IT'S TYRANNY!

ALTHOUGH STUPENDOUS MAN COULD EASILY READ THE ASSIGNMENT WITH STUPENDOUS HIGH-SPEED VISION, THE MASKED MAN OF MIGHT HAS A BOLDER PLAN!

WITH STUPENDOUS POWERS OF REASONING, THE CAPED COMBATANT CONCLUDES THERE'S NO NEED FOR HOMEWORK IF THERE'S NO SCHOOL TOMORROW!

A BLINDING BOLT OF BLAZING CRIMSON CAREENS ACROSS THE SKY! IT'S STUPENDOUS MAN!

SECONDS LATER, THE AMAZING MARVEL ALIGHTS UPON AN OBSERVATORY TELESCOPE AT MOUNT PALOMAR!

WITH STUPENDOUS STRENGTH, STUPENDOUS MAN CAREFULLY UNSCREWS THE GIANT LENS...

...AND BLASTS INTO SPACE WITH IT!

STUPENDOUS MAN CIRCLES THE EARTH WITH A 200-INCH TELESCOPE LENS!

ALIGNED PERFECTLY WITH THE SUN, THE MAGNIFYING LENS FOCUSES THE TERRIBLE SOLAR ENERGY...

...AND FRIES A CERTAIN ELEMENTARY SCHOOL CLEAN OFF THE MAP!

NOW MILD-MANNERED CALVIN HAS NO NEED TO DO HIS HOMEWORK EVER AGAIN! LIBERTY PREVAILS!
HOW'S YOUR HOMEWORK COMING, CALVIN?

UH OH, IT'S MY ARCH-NEMESIS, MOM-LADY! SHE CAN'T DISCOVER MY SECRET IDENTITY!
CALVIN? ARE YOU DOING YOUR HOMEWORK IN THERE?

QUICKLY, STUPENDOUS MAN LEAPS INTO THE CLOSET TO CHANGE BACK INTO HIS 6-YEAR-OLD ALTER EGO, MILD-MANNERED CALVIN!

CALVIN? ARE YOU IN HERE?
UNFORTUNATELY, STUPENDOUS MAN'S CAPE IS CAUGHT IN MILD-MANNERED CALVIN'S ZIPPER! CURSES!

THIS IS GOING TO BE A GOOD ONE, I CAN TELL.
GEEZ, MOM! CAN'T A GUY HAVE A LITTLE PRIVACY?!

AND WHY, MAY I ASK, ARE YOU STANDING IN YOUR UNDERWEAR IN THE CLOSET?
OH, NO REASON. UM... I WAS HOT.

YOU'RE SUPPOSED TO BE DOING YOUR HOMEWORK!
I DON'T NEED TO DO IT NOW, THANKS TO STUPENDOUS MAN!

OH YEAH?

IT WAS GREAT! HE FRIED THE SCHOOL WITH A BIG MAGNIFYING LENS IN SPACE! I'M SURE IT WILL BE IN ALL THE PAPERS TOMORROW.

BOY, SHE'LL BE IN TROUBLE WHEN SHE GIVES ME MY COSTUME BACK. BIG TROUBLE.

Calvin and HobbEs
by WATTERSON

I'M HO-OME!

HI, CALVIN. WHATCHA DOIN'?
OOF, GET THIS BIG LUMMOX OFF ME.

LOOK AT YOU! YOU DIDN'T EVEN CHANGE OUT OF YOUR SCHOOL CLOTHES!
HOW COULD I ?! I DIDN'T EVEN GET IN THE DOOR!

EVERY DAY THIS MANIAC IS SO GLAD TO SEE ME THAT HE BLASTS OUT LIKE A BIG ORANGE TORPEDO! A DOG WILL JUST WAG ITS TAIL, BUT OF COURSE A TIGER HAS TO POUNCE ON YOU! STUPID ANIMAL!

HE POUNCES ON YOU?
OH, AND DON'T THINK HE DOESN'T ENJOY THE CUNNING AND TREACHERY OF IT ALL! TIGERS LIVE FOR THE THRILL OF A SNEAK ATTACK! IT'S THEIR EVIL NATURE!
WATTERSON

HE'S JUST SITTING THERE.
OH, SURE, BIG DISGUISE! LIKE NO ONE CAN FATHOM THE SAVAGE MIND OF A JUNGLE CAT! HA! HE'S A KILLER TO THE CORE!

I WISH MY PARENTS WOULD MOVE. MY DIARY IS GETTING WEIRDER EVERY DAY.
YEAH, YOU KNOW WHO I'M TALKING ABOUT! WIPE OFF THAT GRIN OR I'LL DO IT FOR YOU!

I'VE GOT AN IDEA, DAD.

MAYBE I'D GET BETTER GRADES IF YOU OFFERED ME $1 FOR EVERY "D", $5 FOR EVERY "C", $10 FOR EVERY "B", AND $50 FOR EVERY "A"!

I'M NOT GOING TO **BRIBE** YOU, CALVIN. YOU SHOULD APPLY YOURSELF FOR YOUR OWN GOOD.

RATS. I THOUGHT I COULD MAKE AN EASY FOUR BUCKS.
WATTERSON

HELLO? VALLEY HARDWARE? YES, I'M CALLING TO SEE IF YOU SELL BLASTING CAPS, DETONATORS, TIMERS AND WIRE.

JUST THE WIRE? OK, FORGET IT. DO YOU RENT BULLDOZERS OR BACKHOES?
WATTERSON

NO, NO, A ROTOTILLER WON'T DO AT ALL. I NEED SOMETHING MORE LIKE A WRECKING BALL. DO YOU KNOW WHERE I COULD GET ANYTHING LIKE THAT? NO? OK, GOODBYE.

LOOKS LIKE ANOTHER BORING DAY, HOBBES.

I CAN'T SLEEP, HOBBES. I'VE BEEN THINKING.
WHAT ABOUT?

WELL, SUPPOSE THERE'S NO AFTERLIFE. THAT WOULD MEAN ***THIS*** LIFE IS ALL YOU GET.

AND ***THAT*** WOULD MEAN I'M SITTING HERE IN BED AS PRECIOUS MOMENTS OF MY ALL-TOO-SHORT LIFE DISAPPEAR FOREVER.

HONEY, WAKE UP. DO YOU HEAR THE TELEVISION ON?
WATTERSON

Calvin and Hobbes

by WATTERSON

GOSH, IT'S 1:30 AND I'M STILL AWAKE.

THE STRANGEST THING HAPPENED TO ME A FEW MINUTES AGO.
OH? WHAT?

I WAS MINDING MY OWN BUSINESS, WHEN SUDDENLY I WAS ZAPPED INTO SOME SORT OF SPACE VOID VORTEX!

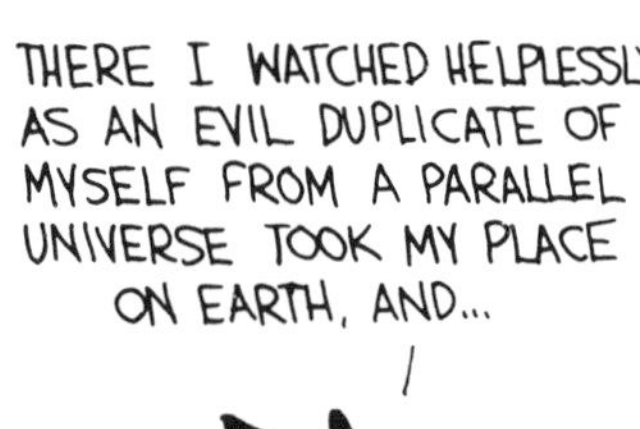
THERE I WATCHED HELPLESSLY AS AN EVIL DUPLICATE OF MYSELF FROM A PARALLEL UNIVERSE TOOK MY PLACE ON EARTH, AND...

WHAT HAVE YOU DONE **NOW**?
NO, NO, SEE, IT WASN'T **ME**...
WATTERSON

HEH HEH HEH!

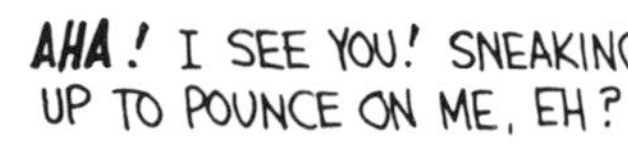
AHA! I SEE YOU! SNEAKING UP TO POUNCE ON ME, EH?

PHOOEY.
YOU SEE WHY **MOST** TIGERS DON'T CHUCKLE TO THEMSELVES.
WATTERSON

WANT TO PLAY A GREAT GAME I INVENTED?
OK.

IT'S CALLED "GROSS OUT." YOU SAY THE GROSSEST THING YOU CAN IMAGINE, AND THEN I TRY TO THINK OF SOMETHING EVEN GROSSER.

WHOEVER COMES UP WITH THE GROSSEST THING GETS A POINT, AND WE PLAY UNTIL SOMEONE GETS 50 POINTS, OK?

I THINK I ALREADY KNOW WHO'S GOING TO WIN.
IT'S WEIRD. NOBODY HAS EVER PLAYED A WHOLE GAME WITH ME.
WATTERSON

Calvin and Hobbes
by WATTERSON
WOW, HONEY, YOU'RE MISSING A BEAUTIFUL SUNSET OUT HERE!

I'LL COUNT TO 10, AND THEN... POW!

DAD, HOW COME OLD PHOTOGRAPHS ARE ALWAYS BLACK AND WHITE? DIDN'T THEY HAVE COLOR FILM BACK THEN?

SURE THEY DID. IN FACT, THOSE OLD PHOTOGRAPHS ARE IN COLOR. IT'S JUST THE WORLD WAS BLACK AND WHITE THEN.

REALLY?
YEP. THE WORLD DIDN'T TURN COLOR UNTIL SOMETIME IN THE 1930s, AND IT WAS PRETTY GRAINY COLOR FOR A WHILE, TOO.

THAT'S REALLY WEIRD.
WELL, TRUTH IS STRANGER THAN FICTION.

BUT THEN WHY ARE OLD PAINTINGS IN COLOR?! IF THE WORLD WAS BLACK AND WHITE, WOULDN'T ARTISTS HAVE PAINTED IT THAT WAY?
NOT NECESSARILY. A LOT OF GREAT ARTISTS WERE INSANE.

BUT...BUT HOW COULD THEY HAVE PAINTED IN COLOR ANYWAY? WOULDN'T THEIR PAINTS HAVE BEEN SHADES OF GRAY BACK THEN?
OF COURSE, BUT THEY TURNED COLORS LIKE EVERYTHING ELSE DID IN THE '30s.

SO WHY DIDN'T OLD BLACK AND WHITE PHOTOS TURN COLOR TOO?
BECAUSE THEY WERE COLOR PICTURES OF BLACK AND WHITE, REMEMBER?

THE WORLD IS A COMPLICATED PLACE, HOBBES.
WHENEVER IT SEEMS THAT WAY, I TAKE A NAP IN A TREE AND WAIT FOR DINNER.
WATTERSON

WHILE YOU'RE THERE, COULD YOU RESEARCH BATS TOO, AND MAKE COPIES OF ALL THE INFORMATION YOU FIND, AND MAYBE UNDERLINE THE IMPORTANT PARTS FOR ME, AND SORT OF OUTLINE IT, SO I WOULDN'T HAVE TO READ IT ALL?

WHAT AM I GOING TO DO ABOUT THIS REPORT ON BATS? YOU'VE GOT TO HELP ME, HOBBES!

OK, ... UM, FIRST LET'S MAKE A LIST OF WHAT WE KNOW.
YEAH! THAT'S A GOOD WAY TO START! GREAT!

NUMBER ONE: WHAT ARE BATS?
THEY'RE BUGS, AREN'T THEY? YEAH, PUT THAT DOWN.

#1 Bats = Bugs
ARE YOU SURE?
THEY FLY, RIGHT? THEY'RE UGLY AND HAIRY, RIGHT? C'MON, THIS IS TAKING ALL DAY!

I THINK WE'VE GOT ENOUGH INFORMATION NOW, DON'T YOU?
ALL WE HAVE IS ONE "FACT" YOU MADE UP.

THAT'S PLENTY. BY THE TIME WE ADD AN INTRODUCTION, A FEW ILLUSTRATIONS, AND A CONCLUSION, IT WILL LOOK LIKE A GRADUATE THESIS.

BESIDES, I'VE GOT A SECRET WEAPON THAT WILL **GUARANTEE** ME A GOOD GRADE! NO TEACHER CAN RESIST **THIS**!
WHAT IS IT?

A CLEAR PLASTIC BINDER! PRETTY PROFESSIONAL LOOKING, EH?
I DON'T WANT CO-AUTHOR CREDIT ON THIS, OK?

HI SUSIE! DID YOU WRITE YOUR REPORT?
YEAH, I SPENT ALL LAST EVENING ON IT. DID YOU?

WELL, WHEN YOU KNOW AS MUCH AS **I** DO, IT DOESN'T TAKE AS LONG. MINE TOOK ABOUT 15 MINUTES.
15 MINUTES?! LET'S SEE.
I GUESS YOU WON'T BE SETTING THE GRADE CURVE **THIS** TIME, SUSIE! READ IT AND WEEP.
"BATS: THE BIG BUG SCOURGE OF THE SKIES."

NOTE THE PROFESSIONAL CLEAR PLASTIC BINDER.
BATS AREN'T **BUGS**!

"DUSK! WITH A CREEPY, TINGLING SENSATION, YOU HEAR THE FLUTTERING OF LEATHERY WINGS! BATS! WITH GLOWING RED EYES AND GLISTENING FANGS, THESE UNSPEAKABLE GIANT BUGS DROP ONTO..."

SHE SAYS I OBVIOUSLY DID NO RESEARCH WHATSOEVER ON BATS AND THAT MY SCIENTIFIC ILLUSTRATION LOOKS LIKE I TRACED THE BATMAN LOGO AND ADDED FANGS!

Calvin and HOBBES
by WATTERSON
I'VE BEEN THINKING, HOBBES.

ON A WEEKEND?
WELL, IT WASN'T ON PURPOSE..

I BELIEVE HISTORY IS A FORCE.

ITS UNALTERABLE TIDE SWEEPS ALL PEOPLE AND INSTITUTIONS ALONG ITS UNRELENTING PATH. EVERYTHING AND EVERYONE SERVES HISTORY'S SINGLE PURPOSE.

AND WHAT IS THAT PURPOSE?
WHY, TO PRODUCE ME, OF COURSE! I'M THE END RESULT OF HISTORY.

YOU?
THINK OF IT! THOUSANDS OF GENERATIONS LIVED AND DIED TO PRODUCE MY EXACT, SPECIFIC PARENTS, WHOSE REASON FOR BEING, OBVIOUSLY, WAS TO PRODUCE ME.

ALL HISTORY UP TO THIS POINT HAS BEEN SPENT PREPARING THE WORLD FOR MY PRESENCE.
HMM, 4½ BILLION YEARS PROBABLY WASN'T LONG ENOUGH.

NOW I'M HERE, AND HISTORY IS VINDICATED.
SO NOW THAT HISTORY'S BROUGHT YOU, WHAT ARE YOU GOING TO DO?

OOH, YOU WASCAWWY WABBIT!
WATTERSON

Calvin and HOBBES

by WATTERSON

HI SUSIE. WHAT DID YOU BRING FOR LUNCH TODAY?
A SWISS CHEESE AND KETCHUP SANDWICH.

IT'S MY VERY FAVORITE, TOO, SO I DON'T WANT TO HEAR WHAT GROSS THING YOU BROUGHT.
RELAX, SUSIE. I BOUGHT THE CAFETERIA LUNCH TODAY.

GOOD.
IT APPEARS TO BE CIGAR BUTTS IN A GALLSTONE SAUCE.

THAT'S BEANY-WIENIES!
REALLY? OH GROSS.
WATTERSON

HELLO?
HI, DAD. IT'S ME, CALVIN.

YOU'RE SUPPOSED TO BE AT SCHOOL!
I AM AT SCHOOL.

ARE YOU ALL RIGHT? WHAT'S THE MATTER? WHY ARE YOU CALLING?

I TOLD THE TEACHER I HAD TO GO TO THE BATHROOM. QUICK, WHAT'S 11+7?
WATTERSON

I WAS READING ABOUT HOW COUNTLESS SPECIES ARE BEING PUSHED TOWARD EXTINCTION BY MAN'S DESTRUCTION OF FORESTS.

SOMETIMES I THINK THE SUREST SIGN THAT INTELLIGENT LIFE EXISTS ELSEWHERE IN THE UNIVERSE IS THAT NONE OF IT HAS TRIED TO CONTACT US.
WATTERSON

WHAT ARE YOU **DOING**?! YOU'RE GOING TO BE LATE FOR SCHOOL! HURRY UP AND PUT YOUR CLOTHES ON RIGHT!
IT'S SAD HOW SOME PEOPLE CAN'T HANDLE A LITTLE VARIETY.
WATTERSON

I WONDER WHY MAN WAS PUT ON EARTH. WHAT'S OUR PURPOSE? WHY ARE WE HERE?

TIGER FOOD.

WATTERSON

Z

Z

SNAP

A LITTLE HIGH-STRUNG, ARE WE?
WE TIGERS CALL IT LIGHTNING QUICK REFLEXES.
WATTERSON

Calvin and HOBBES

by WATTERSON

SIGHHHH...

HEY! WHOA! WHOAA!

WAHH!

BAM
CALVIN, QUIT BANGING AROUND!

OW! WHAT AM I DOING ON THE CEILING?

HMM... NOTHING ELSE FELL UP. JUST ME. THIS IS VERY STRANGE.

EVEN IF I TRY TO JUMP TO THE FLOOR, I LAND BACK ON THE CEILING! MY PERSONAL GRAVITY MUST HAVE REVERSED POLARITY!

YOU'D THINK THIS WOULD BE THE TYPE OF THING WE'D LEARN ABOUT IN SCIENCE CLASS, BUT NO, WE LEARN ABOUT CIRRUS CLOUDS.

HAVING MY PERSONAL GRAVITY POLARITY REVERSED IS A REAL NUISANCE. HOW AM I GOING TO GET UP TO THE FLOOR?

THERE'S NOT ANYTHING ON THE CEILING THAT I COULD EVEN CLIMB UP.
HOW AM I SUPPOSED TO DO MY HOMEWORK WHEN I'M TRAPPED ON THE CEILING? IT'S IMPOSSIBLE.

MOM AND DAD WON'T BE TOO HAPPY ABOUT **THIS**. NO SIR.

DAD WILL HAVE TO BOLT MY BED TO THE CEILING TONIGHT, AND MOM WILL HAVE TO STAND ON A STEPLADDER TO HAND ME DINNER.

THEN I'LL HAVE TO HOLD MY PLATE UPSIDE-DOWN ABOVE MY HEAD AND SCRAPE THE FOOD OFF THE UNDERSIDE! AND IF I SPILL ANYTHING, IT WILL FLY 10 FEET UP TO THE FLOOR AND SPLOT!

THIS IS GOING TO BE THE MOST FUN I'VE EVER HAD!

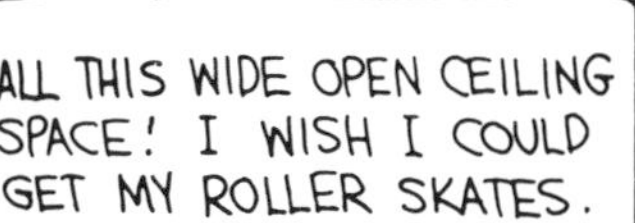
ALL THIS WIDE OPEN CEILING SPACE! I WISH I COULD GET MY ROLLER SKATES.

HEY, MAYBE I CAN CLIMB UP THIS BOOKCASE AND WHEN I GET TO THE BOTTOM SHELF, LEAP TO A CHAIR!

THEN I CAN PULL MYSELF ACROSS TO OTHER PIECES OF FURNITURE AND WORK MY WAY TO MY TOY CHEST.

...I CAN HEAR MOM NOW: "HOW ON EARTH DID YOU GET SNEAKER PRINTS ON THE UNDERSIDE OF EACH SHELF?!"

THERE! I THINK I CAN JUMP TO THAT CHAIR AND HANG ONTO THE BACK.

GEERONIMOOO!

¡AAAAOHW

WHAM!
GREAT. JUST GREAT.
CALVIN, QUIT BANGING AROUND!

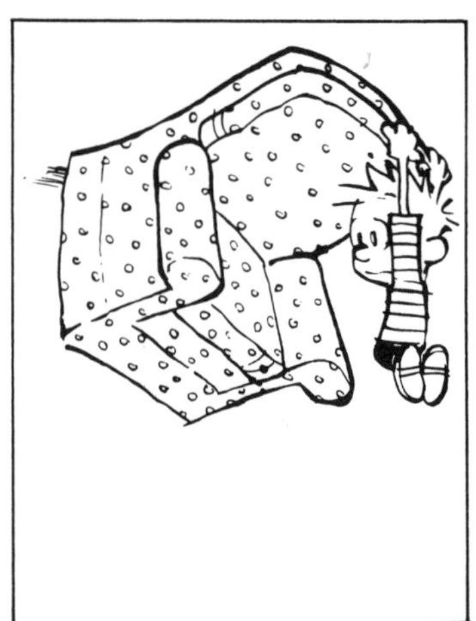

RRG!
MMF!

GETTING ANY HOMEWORK DONE, OR ARE YOU JUST RUINING FURNITURE?
MAYBE I'M HANGING HERE FOR DEAR LIFE! EVER THINK OF THAT?

I'M TELLING YOU, MY PERSONAL GRAVITY REVERSED ITS POLARITY! I FALL UP NOW!

I'VE BEEN TRAPPED ON THE CEILING! I COULDN'T DO MY HOMEWORK UP THERE! MY DESK IS ON THE FLOOR!

YOU SHOULD BE GLAD I WASN'T OUTSIDE WHEN IT HAPPENED, OR I'D BE SAILING THROUGH THE IONOSPHERE!

RIGHT. NOW I DON'T WANT TO HEAR ANY MORE NONSENSE UNTIL YOU'RE THROUGH WITH YOUR HOMEWORK, UNDERSTAND?
DON'T LET GO! DON'T LET GO!

IT'S... IT'S A MIRACLE! MY PERSONAL GRAVITY IS BACK TO NORMAL!
GLAD TO HEAR IT. NOW DO YOUR MATH.

YOU BET, MOM. BOY, WHAT A RELIEF TO BE PULLED DOWN INSTEAD OF UP!
I'LL CHECK YOUR PROGRESS IN A LITTLE BIT.

UH OH.

THIS HAS BEEN A MOST PECULIAR AFTERNOON.

I'VE GOT TO GET OUT-SIDE BEFORE I GROW BIGGER!

I SUPPOSE I SHOULD GET MY PITUITARY GLAND CHECKED.

I KNOW! I'LL RUN DOWN-TOWN AND FIND DAD AT WORK! MAYBE HE CAN HELP!

HMM... NOW WHICH BUILDING DOES DAD WORK IN? THEY ALL LOOK THE SAME.

...WELL, MAYBE DAD CAN FIND **ME**.

WELL? HOW'S YOUR MATH COMING ALONG?
I'VE ALMOST STARTED!

OH BROTHER! ANOTHER "DISCUSSION" ABOUT MY STUDY HABITS AND THE IMPORTANCE OF HOMEWORK.

I TRIED EXPLAINING THAT IT'S HARD TO STUDY WHEN ONE'S SIZE SUDDENLY STARTS INCREASING, BUT DOES SHE CARE?! HAH!

NO, IT'S JUST BLAH BLAH BLAH, LIKE IT'S ALL MY FAULT! MOM'S NEVER BEEN AS BIG AS A GALAXY, SO SHE CAN'T UNDERSTAND HOW ANYONE ELSE COULD BE! SHEEESH.

OOPS, IT LOOKS LIKE SHE'S WRAPPING UP. BETTER START NODDING.
GOOD. I'M GLAD WE HAD THIS LITTLE TALK.

DOING HOMEWORK?
YEAHHHH... BOY, YOU MISSED THE SHOW.

I GOT A BIG LECTURE FROM MOM JUST BECAUSE I GOT STUCK ON THE CEILING AND THEN GREW SO BIG I FELL OFF THE PLANET WHEN I WAS SUPPOSED TO BE DOING MY MATH!

GEE, THAT'S NOT VERY FAIR.
YOU SAID IT. HERE, HOW ABOUT HELPING ME HURRY UP WITH THESE PROBLEMS?
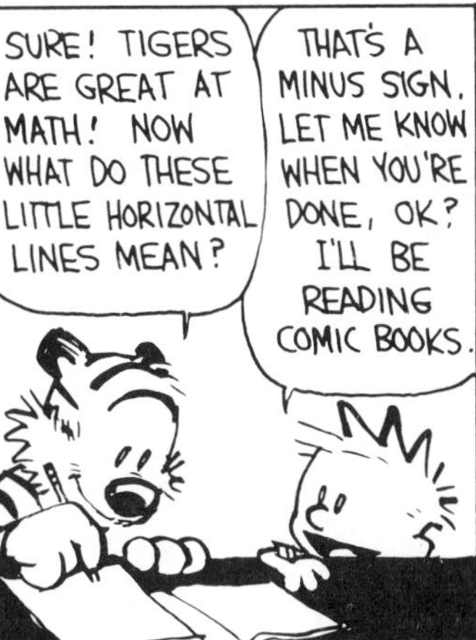
SURE! TIGERS ARE GREAT AT MATH! NOW WHAT DO THESE LITTLE HORIZONTAL LINES MEAN?
THAT'S A MINUS SIGN. LET ME KNOW WHEN YOU'RE DONE, OK? I'LL BE READING COMIC BOOKS.

Calvin and Hobbes
by WATTERSON
OUT IN THE FARTHEST REACHES OF THE GALAXY ZOOMS INTERPLANETARY EXPLORER, SPACEMAN SPIFF!

OOH, NICE SCENERY!

THE MUCK MONSTERS OF MORDO ARE CLOSING IN ON OUR HERO! A FIERY FLASH OF FATALITY-FLARE MISSES BY MERE MICROMIPS!

SPIFF'S DESPERATE GAMBIT: TO FLY THROUGH THE RINGS OF PLANET ZK-5 BELOW! OUR HERO THROTTLES THE THRUSTERS AND DIVES!

IT WORKS! THE MUCK MONSTERS VEER OFF, AFRAID TO FOLLOW THE FEARLESS SPIFF INTO THE FROZEN FRAGMENTS OF ICE AND ROCK!

SWERVING LEFT, RIGHT, UP, AND DOWN, THE AMAZING SPACEMAN SPIFF PILOTS AROUND EACH HURLING MISSILE! WHAT SKILL! WHAT FORTITU...

POW!
OH NO! OUR HERO IS GOING DOWN!!

Got 'im! Heh heh!
THOSE DARN LITTLE GUYS ARE HARD TO HIT, AREN'T THEY?
I HATE PLAYING "DODGE BALL" IN GYM CLASS.
WATTERSON

WHEN ARE WE GOING TO GET A CHRISTMAS TREE?
OH, I DUNNO. PROBABLY A LITTLE AFTER NEW YEAR'S.

AFTER NEW YEAR'S?
SURE. WE CAN JUST GO UP THE STREET AND PICK THE BEST TREE FROM THE NEIGHBORS' DRIVEWAYS.

WHAT?!
SOMETIMES THERE'S STILL TINSEL ON THE TREE TOO, SO YOU DON'T EVEN HAVE TO DECORATE IT! WE'LL SAVE TIME AND MONEY!

OK, WHAT DID YOUR DAD TELL YOU THIS TIME?

YES, CALVIN? YOU HAVE A QUESTION?
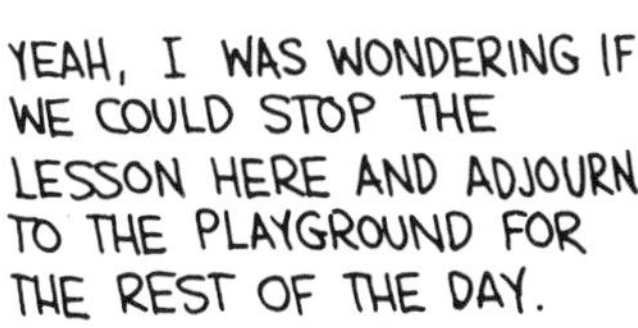
YEAH, I WAS WONDERING IF WE COULD STOP THE LESSON HERE AND ADJOURN TO THE PLAYGROUND FOR THE REST OF THE DAY.

OF COURSE NOT. NOW THEN, LET'S ALL TURN TO PAGE 24 AND...
MISS WORMWOOD?

YES?
HOW ABOUT JUST ME THEN?

FOR "SHOW AND TELL" TODAY, I HAVE SOMETHING THAT WILL ASTOUND AND AMAZE YOU! THIS LITTLE GUY CAN...

HAVE YOU ALL HAD YOUR SHOTS?

Calvin and HOBBES

by WATTERSON

DEAR SANTA,
HOW ARE YOU?
WELL, ENOUGH CHIT CHAT. LET'S GET DOWN TO BUSINESS.
THIS YEAR I WANT...

NO, IT'S TOO MUCH TROUBLE. **FIRST** I'D HAVE TO GET UP. **THEN** I'D HAVE TO PUT ON A COAT. **THEN** I'D HAVE TO FIND MY HAT AND PUT **IT** ON. (SIGH) THEN WE'D RUN AROUND AND I'D GET TIRED, AND WHEN WE CAME IN I'D HAVE TO TAKE ALL THAT STUFF **OFF**. NO WAY.

I'LL TELL YOUR MOM TO TURN YOU TOWARD THE LIGHT AND WATER YOU PERIODICALLY.

Calvin and HOBBES

by WATTERSON

KNOW WHAT THIS IS?

WHAT ARE YOU DOING STILL IN BED?! I'VE CALLED YOU THREE TIMES! YOU'RE GOING TO MISS THE BUS!

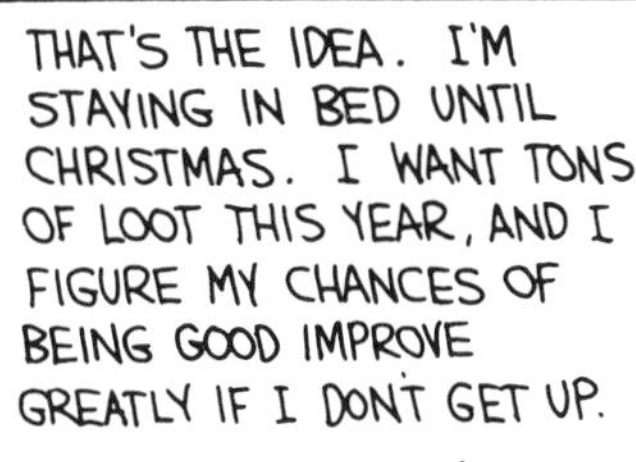
THAT'S THE IDEA. I'M STAYING IN BED UNTIL CHRISTMAS. I WANT TONS OF LOOT THIS YEAR, AND I FIGURE MY CHANCES OF BEING GOOD IMPROVE GREATLY IF I DON'T GET UP.

DISOBEYING YOUR MOTHER AND MISSING THE BUS ISN'T GOOD. IT'S BAD.

THAT DARN SANTA HAS GOT ME EVERY WAY I TURN.

I HATE THIS TIME OF YEAR. I'VE GOT TO BE GOOD FOR TWO MORE WEEKS IF I WANT ANY GOODIES THIS CHRISTMAS! I'LL NEVER MAKE IT.

I TRY TO BE GOOD! I DO! MY HEART IS AS PURE AS DRIVEN SNOW!
IT'S JUST THAT, WELL, SOMETIMES EVENTS BEYOND MY CONTROL CONSPIRE AGAINST ME!

I'M USUALLY AN INNOCENT BYSTAND... HEY, I SAW YOU ROLL YOUR EYES! SO YOU DON'T BELIEVE ME, EH?!
ME??

BY GOLLY, EACH OF YOUR EYES WILL BE ROLLING TOWARD THE OTHER WHEN I'M THROUGH WITH YOU!
HA! I HOPE YOU ASKED SANTA FOR SOME CRUTCHES!
OOF!
ZING

MISERABLE MISCREANT! QUESTION MY INTEGRITY, WILL YOU?
I CAN'T QUESTION IT UNTIL I SEE SOME EVIDENCE OF IT!

AUGHH! I'VE BEEN FIGHTING!
ONLY IN THE LOOSEST SENSE OF THE WORD.

SANTA, HE MADE ME! I DIDN'T MEAN TO FIGHT!
YES HE DID! YES HE DID! HE STARTED IT!

I DID NOT!
DID TOO!
DID NOT!
DID TOO!
LIAR!
LIAR!

FORTUNATELY, I ASKED SANTA FOR SUCH GREAT PRESENTS THAT I CAN WITHSTAND ANY TEMPTATION. I'M BEING AN ABSOLUTE ANGEL.

Calvin and HobbEs

by WATTERSON

WANT TO HELP ME WRITE A BOOK?
SURE. WHAT'S IT ABOUT?

WELL, YOU KNOW WHAT HISTORICAL FICTION IS? THIS IS SORT OF LIKE THAT. I'M WRITING A FICTIONAL AUTOBIOGRAPHY.

IT'S THE STORY OF MY LIFE, BUT WITH A LOT OF PARTS COMPLETELY MADE UP.
WHY WOULD YOU MAKE UP YOUR OWN LIFE?

BECAUSE IN MY BOOK I HAVE A FLAME THROWER!

STILL AND QUIET FELINE FORM, IN THE SUN, ASLEEP AND WARM. HIS TAIL IS LIMP, HIS WHISKERS DROOPED. MAN, WHAT COULD MAKE THIS CAT SO POOPED?

SHEESHH..

HI MOM! I'M MAKING MY OWN NEWSPAPER TO REPORT THE EVENTS OF OUR HOUSEHOLD.
THAT'S NICE.

NOW I'M LOOKING FOR A PAGE ONE LEAD STORY. CAN I INTERVIEW YOU?
SURE.

OK, WHAT ARE YOU CUTTING UP THERE FOR DINNER?
FISH.

KNIFE WIELDING MOTHER HACKS ICHTHYOID! GRIM MELEE IS EVENING RITUAL! SUBURBAN FAMILY DEVOURS VICTIM!
OUT OF THE KITCHEN! OUT! OUT!

HI DAD. I'M MAKING MY OWN NEWSPAPER TO REPORT THE EVENTS OF OUR HOUSEHOLD. WOULD YOU HELP ME OUT?
SURE, WHAT DO YOU NEED?

WELL, YOU CAN TAKE YOUR PICK. EITHER YOU CAN GIVE ME 15 BUCKS TO PAY MY LABOR AND PRODUCTION COSTS...
15 BUCKS?!

...OR YOU CAN BE THE SUBJECT OF A COMIC STRIP CALLED "DOPEY DAD."
WATTERSON

SO IN THE NEXT PANEL, DOPEY DAD YELLS, "IT'S BED-TIME FOR **YOU**, YOUNG MAN!"
HEE HEE! LOOK HOW BIG I MADE HIS MOUTH!

OOH HAHH
OOH HAHH

OOH HAHH
OOH HAHH

OOH HAHH
OOH HAHHH
WATTERSON

I WISH WE'D GED AD AQUARIUB!

WHAT STORY WOULD YOU LIKE TONIGHT, CALVIN?
HAMSTER HUEY AND THE GOOEY KABLOOIE!

OH NO, NOT **AGAIN**! THAT'S WHAT YOU HEAR **EVERY** NIGHT! LET'S READ SOMETHING DIFFERENT.
I WANT HAMSTER HUEY! I WANT HAMSTER HUEY!

C'MON, WE'LL READ A **NEW** STORY TONIGHT. YOU'LL LIKE IT, I PROMISE.
NO I WON'T! I'LL STAY AWAKE UNTIL MORNING IF YOU DON'T READ HAMSTER HUEY!

I DIDN'T REMEMBER HAMSTER HUEY HAVING QUITE THAT SARCASTIC TONE OF VOICE.
OR DOING EVERYTHING SO **FAST**.
WATTERSON

CALVIN AND HOBBES
by WATTERSON
Christmas Eve
ON WINDOW PANES, THE ICY FROST
LEAVES FEATHERED PATTERNS, CRISSED & CROSSED,
BUT IN OUR HOUSE THE CHRISTMAS TREE
IS DECORATED FESTIVELY
WITH TINY DOTS OF COLORED LIGHT
THAT COZY UP THIS WINTER NIGHT.
CHRISTMAS SONGS, FAMILIAR, SLOW,
PLAY SOFTLY ON THE RADIO.
POPS AND HISSES FROM THE FIRE
WHISTLE WITH THE BELLS AND CHOIR.
MY TIGER IS NOW FAST ASLEEP
ON HIS BACK AND DREAMING DEEP.
WHEN THE FIRE MAKES HIM HOT,
HE TURNS TO WARM WHATEVER'S NOT.
PROPPED AGAINST HIM ON THE RUG,
I GIVE MY FRIEND A GENTLE HUG.
TOMORROW'S WHAT I'M WAITING FOR,
BUT I CAN WAIT A LITTLE MORE.

HA HA! IT'S CHRISTMAS! **HURRY UP, MOM AND DAD!** IT'S ALMOST DAWN!
HERE, I GOT YOU A PRESENT.

YOU GOT ME A PRESENT? GOSH HOBBES, HOW NICE!
I PICKED IT OUT MYSELF! OPEN IT!

WHY, IT'S... IT'S THREE CANS OF... UH... SALMON. UM, THANKS, HOBBES.
YOU'RE WELCOME!

GEE, I DIDN'T GET **YOU** A PRESENT. I FEEL TERRIBLE.
I THOUGHT OF THAT. SEE, YOU COULD GIVE ME MINE **BACK**! THAT WOULD BE A **GOOD** PRESENT!

WELL THEN, HERE! MERRY CHRISTMAS, HOBBES!
WHY, THANK YOU! IT'S JUST WHAT I WANTED! MERRY CHRISTMAS!
CALVIN, DID YOU KNOCK THESE CANS OVER IN THE PANTRY?

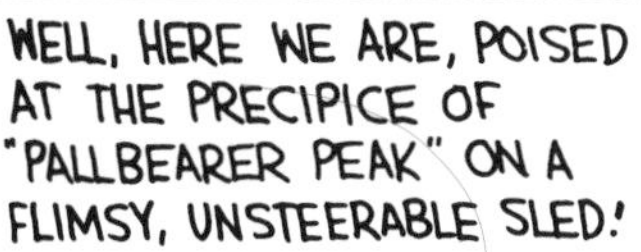
WELL, HERE WE ARE, POISED AT THE PRECIPICE OF "PALLBEARER PEAK" ON A FLIMSY, UNSTEERABLE SLED!

THE MIND RECOILS IN HORROR TO IMAGINE THE AWFUL DESCENT! YES, IT'S A THOUSAND FOOT VERTICAL DROP ONTO A BOULDER FIELD LINED WITH PRICKER BUSHES! IT'S A JOURNEY CALCULATED TO EXCEED THE HUMAN CAPACITY FOR BLINDING FEAR!

READY TO GO?
READY!

NEW HAT, DAD?
YEP.

I LIKE IT.
THANK YOU. SO DO I.

AAUGH!
YOU'RE GOING TO BE LATE FOR WORK, DAD!

YOU DON'T LIKE MY "SNOWMAN HOUSE OF HORROR," DO YOU?!

I SEE YOU, HOBBES! MAN, WHAT A LOUSY SHOT! TIGERS CAN'T THROW WORTH A..

SMACK!

I JUST THREW THE FIRST ONE SO YOU'D TURN AROUND.

A NEW DECADE IS COMING UP.
YEAH, BIG DEAL! HMPH.

WHERE ARE THE FLYING CARS? WHERE ARE THE MOON COLONIES? WHERE ARE THE PERSONAL ROBOTS AND THE ZERO GRAVITY BOOTS, HUH? YOU CALL THIS A NEW DECADE?! YOU CALL THIS THE FUTURE?? HA!

WHERE ARE THE ROCKET PACKS? WHERE ARE THE DISINTEGRATION RAYS? WHERE ARE THE FLOATING CITIES?

FRANKLY, I'M NOT SURE PEOPLE HAVE THE BRAINS TO MANAGE THE TECHNOLOGY THEY'VE GOT.
I MEAN, LOOK AT THIS! WE STILL HAVE WEATHER?! GIVE ME A BREAK!

FOR YOUR INFORMATION, I'M ***STAYING*** LIKE THIS, AND EVERYONE ELSE CAN JUST GET ***USED*** TO IT! IF PEOPLE DON'T LIKE ME THE WAY I AM, WELL, **TOUGH** BEANS! IT'S A FREE COUNTRY! I DON'T NEED ANYONE'S PERMISSION TO BE THE WAY I WANT! THIS IS HOW I AM - TAKE IT OR LEAVE IT!

BEFORE GOING DOWN A STEEP HILL LIKE THIS, ONE SHOULD ALWAYS GIVE HIS SLED A SAFETY CHECK.
RIGHT.

SEAT BELTS?
NONE.
SIGNALS?
NONE.

BRAKES?
NONE.
STEERING?
NONE.

WHEEEEEEE

HOW COLD IS IT OUTSIDE?
I DON'T KNOW. WHY DON'T YOU CHECK?

IT'S PRETTY DARN COLD, I'D SAY.
LET ME SHOW YOU AN INTERESTING GADGET THAT'S HANGING OUTSIDE THE WINDOW.

THIS IS THE PART OF WINTER I LIKE BEST... WHEN YOU COME INSIDE, FREEZING COLD AND SOAKED...

...AND YOU PUT ON FRESH DRY CLOTHES, AND RUN UP TO THE WARM KITCHEN, WHERE MOM'S GOT A STEAMING MUG OF HOT CHOCOLATE WAITING FOR YOU!

MOM? ... MOM?? HEY MOM!

"CALVIN, I'M NEXT DOOR. DON'T HAVE ANYTHING TO EAT, OR YOU'LL SPOIL YOUR APPETITE. MOM."
IT'S GOING TO BE A LONG, COLD, DARK WINTER.
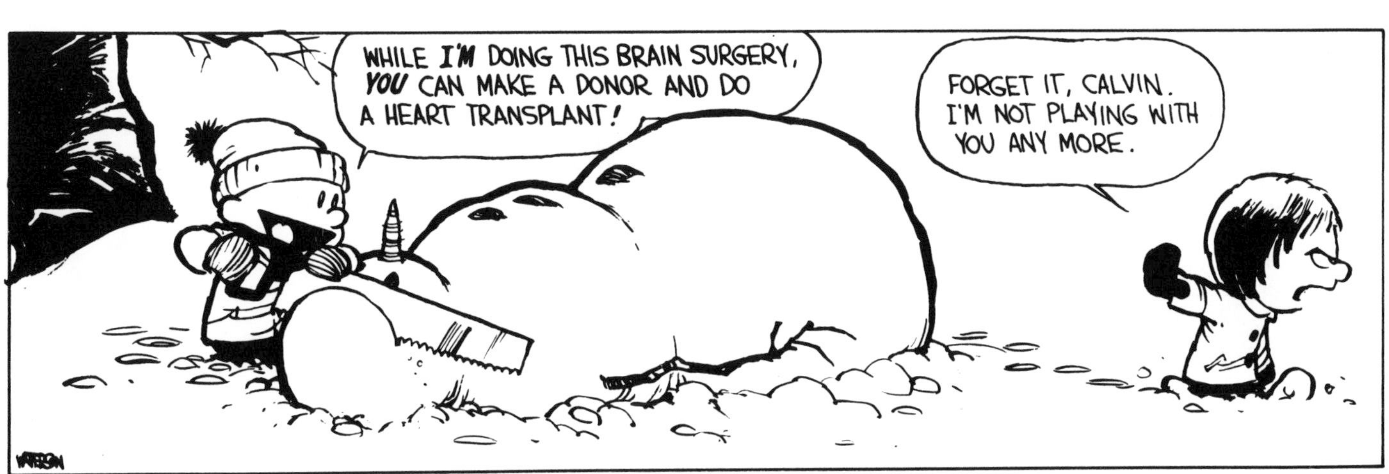
WHILE I'M DOING THIS BRAIN SURGERY, YOU CAN MAKE A DONOR AND DO A HEART TRANSPLANT!
FORGET IT, CALVIN. I'M NOT PLAYING WITH YOU ANY MORE.

Calvin and Hobbes

by WATTERSON

LOOK, HOBBES! MY NEWEST INVENTION!
ISN'T THAT YOUR TRANS-MOGRIFIER?

IT *WAS*, BUT I MADE SOME MODIFICATIONS. SEE, THE BOX IS ON ITS SIDE NOW. IT'S A DUPLICATOR!
AH.

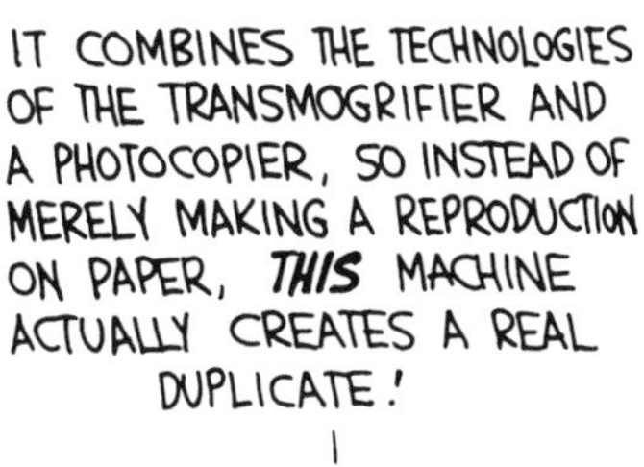
IT COMBINES THE TECHNOLOGIES OF THE TRANSMOGRIFIER AND A PHOTOCOPIER, SO INSTEAD OF MERELY MAKING A REPRODUCTION ON PAPER, *THIS* MACHINE ACTUALLY CREATES A REAL DUPLICATE!

SO OUR FINANCIAL WORRIES ARE OVER?
AND COUNTERFEITING IS JUST *ONE* OF ITS MANY USES AROUND THE HOME!
DUPLICATOR

HAVE YOU TESTED YOUR DUPLICATOR MACHINE YET?
I WAS JUST ABOUT TO. YOU CAN HELP.

OH BOY! WHAT WILL WE DUPLICATE FIRST?
ME!

YOU??
YEAH! MOM WANTS ME TO CLEAN MY ROOM, SO I'LL DU-PLICATE MYSELF AND LET THE DU-PLICATE DO THE WORK! SMART, HUH?

I CAN PICTURE THE LOOK ON YOUR PARENTS' FACES WHEN THEY FIND OUT THEY'VE SUDDENLY HAD TWINS.
TWINS, HECK! THIS SUMMER I CAN MAKE A WHOLE BASEBALL TEAM!

OK HOBBES, PRESS THE BUTTON AND DUPLICATE ME.
ARE YOU SURE THIS IS SUCH A GOOD IDEA?

BROTHER! YOU DOUBTING THOMASES GET IN THE WAY OF MORE SCIENTIFIC AD-VANCES WITH YOUR STUPID ETHICAL QUESTIONS! THIS IS A *BRILLIANT* IDEA! HIT THE BUTTON, WILL YA?

I'D HATE TO BE ACCUSED OF INHIBITING SCIENTIFIC PROGRESS... HERE YOU GO.
BOINK
BUTTON

SCIENTIFIC PROGRESS GOES "BOINK"?
IT WORKED! IT WORKED! I'M A GENIUS!
NO YOU'RE NOT, YOU LIAR! *I* INVENTED THIS!

THE DUPLICATOR WORKED! HOBBES, MEET MY DUPLICATE!
OOG. I'M NOT SURE I'M READY FOR THIS.
HEY, NICE ROOM.

OK, DUPE! HOBBES AND I ARE GOING OUT TO PLAY. YOU CLEAN MY ROOM, AND WHEN YOU'RE DONE, I'VE GOT SOME HOMEWORK YOU CAN DO, TOO.
WHAT?!

FORGET IT, BUB! FIND SOME OTHER SUCKER TO DO YOUR DIRTY WORK! LAST ONE OUTSIDE IS A ROTTEN EGG!
HEY! COME BACK HERE!

HE'S A DUPLICATE OF YOU, ALL RIGHT.
WHAT DO YOU MEAN? THIS GUY IS A TOTAL JERK!

WHERE ARE YOU GOING? DID YOU CLEAN YOUR ROOM LIKE I ASKED YOU TO?

I'M GOING OUTSIDE. CALVIN CAN CLEAN HIS OWN ROOM.
I DON'T WANT ANY NONSENSE, CALVIN. GO UPSTAIRS.

CALVIN? I'M NOT CALVIN. I'M HIS DUPLICATE. CALVIN'S IN HIS ROOM.
WHAT DID I JUST SAY? NO NONSENSE, CALVIN! GO CLEAN YOUR ROOM.

BOY, YOU ARE A CRABBY LADY! WHO ARE YOU? CALVIN'S CRUEL GOVERNESS?
THAT DOES IT.

C'MON, HOBBES. WE'D BETTER GO FIND MY DUPLICATE BEFORE HE GETS ME IN TROUBLE.

I'M TELLING YOU, LADY, YOU'VE GOT THE WRONG GUY! I'M A DUPLICATE OF CALVIN! CALVIN'S IN HIS ROOM!
WE'LL SEE ABOUT THAT. GIVE ME YOUR COAT.

SEE, CALVIN? THERE'S NO ONE HERE. NOW THAT'S ENOUGH GAMES. CLEAN YOUR ROOM, OK?
CALVIN?

I DON'T SEE HIM, HOBBES. MAYBE HE'S OUTSIDE, HUH?
WE'D BETTER HURRY. I THINK I HEAR YOUR MOM COMING DOWN THE STAIRS.

CALVIN! WHAT ARE YOU DOING OUTSIDE?! DIDN'T I JUST SEND YOU TO CLEAN YOUR ROOM TWO MINUTES AGO?!
NO.

I DID TOO! NOW GET BACK UPSTAIRS. I'M LOSING MY PATIENCE FOR THIS GAME!
SHE MUST'VE FOUND MY DUPLICATE! C'MON HOBBES, WE'D BETTER HURRY BEFORE HE GETS US IN MORE TROUBLE!

NUMBER THREE, HI! I'M NUMBER TWO!
CHARMED.
DUPLI

MOM SAID SHE SENT ME UPSTAIRS A MINUTE AGO! THAT MUST'VE BEEN MY DUPLICATE!
WHAT A MESS THIS IS TURNING OUT TO BE!

YOU SAID IT! HE GETS IN TROUBLE, BUT I'M THE ONE WHO GETS BLAMED! WE'D BETTER STRAIGHTEN HIM...

AAUGH!

YOUR DUPLICATOR IS A BIG SUCCESS.
ARE YOU KIDDING? IT BURNED OUT AFTER THE FIFTH ONE OF US!
OH NO!

OH NO! MY DUPLICATE MADE DUPLICATES!
HI! WE'RE NUMBERS TWO THROUGH SIX!
HI!
HI!
HI!

HOBBES, WHAT AM I GOING TO DO?!
BETTER TELL YOUR MOM TO PUT OUT THE EXTRA TABLE SETTINGS.

LOOK, YOU GUYS HAVE TO STAY IN HERE AND BE REAL QUIET! IF MY MOM FINDS OUT ABOUT THIS, SHE'LL HAVE A FIT!
STAY HERE?!
NO WAY.
FORGET IT.

I'M THE ORIGINAL! YOU HAVE TO DO WHAT I SAY!
OH YEAH? LET'S PUT IT TO A VOTE.

I DON'T KNOW ABOUT THE REST OF YOU, BUT I'M GOING TO GET SOME COOKIES!
I'M GOING OUTSIDE!
I WONDER WHAT'S ON TV NOW?
YOU GUYS, COME BACK! MOM WILL SEE YOU!

SO WHAT? SO LONG AS WE SPLIT UP AND SHE ONLY SEES ONE OF US AT A TIME, SHE'LL JUST THINK WE'RE YOU!
HA HA HA, HA HA

WHAT A BUNCH OF DEVIOUS LITTLE STINKERS! WHERE'D THEY LEARN TO MISBEHAVE LIKE THAT?!
I THINK WE SHOULD CHECK INTO A HOTEL UNTIL THIS IS OVER.

CALVIN, YOU KNOW YOU'RE NOT ALLOWED TO EAT COOKIES BEFORE DINNER! PUT THOSE AWAY! DID YOU CLEAN YOUR ROOM YET?

I'M NOT CALVIN. I'M A DUPLICATE.
I DON'T WANT TO HEAR ABOUT IT. NOW MOVE!

OOH, SOME DAYS THAT KID OF MINE...

WHAT ARE YOU DOING IN HERE?!
WHY? ARE YOU TAKING A SURVEY?

I'M HOME!
HI.

HI, CALVIN.

HI.
I SAID HI.

HI.
KNOCK IT OFF, CALVIN.
DEAR, HAVE A TALK WITH HIM. HE'S BEEN DRIVING ME CRAZY.

I'M NOT CALVIN. I'M DUPLICATE NUMBER FIVE. DUPLICATE **TWO** WAS HERE YESTERDAY, NOT **ME**. WE'RE ALL TAKING TURNS. NUMBER TWO WILL BE BACK NEXT WEEK, AND YOU CAN ASK HIM TO DO THE PROBLEM ***THEN***.

GUYS? IT'S OK TO COME OUT! IT'S ME, NUMBER FOUR. I'M HOME.

HOW WAS SCHOOL TODAY?
AHH, I GOT SENT TO THE PRINCIPAL'S OFFICE, JUST LIKE NUMBERS TWO AND FIVE DID.

GEEZ, YOU GUYS! EVEN ***I*** DON'T GET SENT TO THE PRINCIPAL EVERY ***DAY***! YOU'RE MAKING ME LOOK BAD!
LOOK, CALVIN, IF YOU DON'T LIKE OUR PERFORMANCE, YOU CAN GO TO SCHOOL ***YOURSELF***!

WHOA, LET'S NOT JUMP TO CONCLUSIONS! I'M JUST SAYING THERE'S ROOM FOR IMPROVEMENT.
HEY FOUR, WERE YOU ABLE TO SWIPE ANY CHALK?
YEAH! THE PRINCIPAL NEVER FRISKED ME!

HOBBES, WE'VE GOT TO GET RID OF THESE DUPLICATES! ALL THEY DO IS GET ME IN TROUBLE!

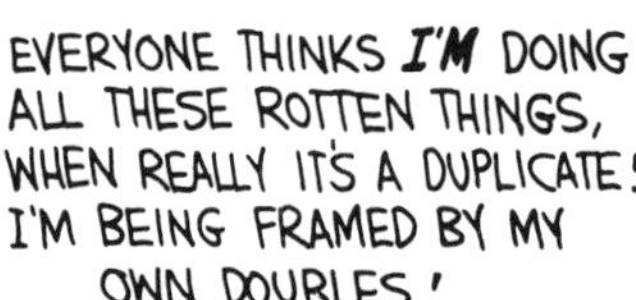
EVERYONE THINKS ***I'M*** DOING ALL THESE ROTTEN THINGS, WHEN REALLY IT'S A DUPLICATE! I'M BEING FRAMED BY MY OWN DOUBLES!

RUN!
HIDE!
OUTTA MY WAY!

IT APPEARS YOU'VE JUST PERPETRATED ANOTHER CRIME.
THE WORST PART IS THAT I DON'T EVEN HAVE THE FUN OF DOING THE STUFF I'M GETTING BLAMED FOR.

ALL RIGHT, WHAT DID YOU GUYS DO ***NOW***?
YOU'D BETTER HIDE, CALVIN! YOUR MOM'S ON THE WARPATH!

CALVIN?
SHE'S COMING! QUICK, GET UNDER THE DUPLICATOR BOX!
DUPLI

THERE YOU ARE! WHAT HAVE YOU GOT TO SAY FOR YOURSELF? I WANT AN EXPLANATION FOR THIS BEHAVIOR!
DUPLICATOR

TELL HER YOU NEED A BIGGER ALLOWANCE!
YEAH! FIVE ***TIMES*** BIGGER!
UM, CAN I GET BACK TO YOU ON THIS, MOM?
NO.

BOY, MOM SURE READ *ME* THE RIOT ACT, DIDN'T SHE?
I HAVE AN IDEA.

PSST, CALVIN! IS THE COAST CLEAR?
DID YOUR MOM GO AWAY YET?
CAN WE COME OUT NOW?

OH NO! YOUR MOM'S COMING BACK!
THERE SHE IS! STAY IN THE BOX, GUYS! KEEP QUIET!
SHH!
YIKES!

HOBBES, YOU'RE A GENIUS!
I DON'T HEAR HER. DO YOU?
HEY, WHAT'S GOING ON OUT THERE?
DUPLICATOR
TRANSMOG-RIFIER

SO LONG, DUPLICATES!
WHAT DO YOU MEAN? WE'RE NOT GOING ANYWH...
TRANSMOG-RIFIER

ZAP!
DUPLICATOR
TRANSM -RIFIE

WHAT DID YOU TRANSMOGRIFY THEM INTO?
WORMS!

WORMS?!
WELL, I DIDN'T WANT THEM TO BE UNHAPPY...
COOL! LOOK AT US!
HA HA! LET'S GO GROSS SOMEONE OUT!

WELL MOM, YOU DON'T NEED TO WORRY ABOUT ME GETTING IN TROUBLE ANY MORE.
OH REALLY?

YUP. SEE, I MADE THESE DUPLICATES OF MYSELF, AND *THEY* WERE THE ONES WHO WERE BAD, NOT ME.
UH HUH...

BUT *NOW* LOOK! I TRANSMOG-RIFIED THEM!
OH CALVIN! DON'T CARRY *WORMS* THROUGH THE HOUSE! OUT! OUT!

WELL THERE! YOU GOT ME IN TROUBLE ONE LAST TIME. I HOPE YOU'RE HAPPY!
YOU'RE SURE YOU DON'T WANT TO PUT US ON YOUR DAD'S DINNER PLATE TONIGHT BEFORE WE GO?

WELL, HOBBES, I GUESS WE LEARNED A VALUABLE LESSON FROM THIS DUPLICATING MESS.

AND THAT IS?
AND THAT IS, UM... IT'S THAT, WELL...

OK, SO WE DIDN'T LEARN ANY BIG LESSON. SUE ME.
LIVE AND DON'T LEARN, THAT'S US.

WHAP!

DID YOU THROW THAT?!?
THROW WHAT?

LET ME SEE YOUR MITTENS! THERE, LOOK! FLECKS OF BARK, PIECES OF GRAVEL, SPOTS OF MUD, AND GRANULES OF ICE! THAT WAS YOUR SNOWBALL, ALL RIGHT!

THAT'S THE PROBLEM WITH HAVING A SIGNATURE STYLE.

HA! YOU MISSED BY A MILE! NYAH NYAHH! THBPTBH!

YES?
YOU'RE DARN LUCKY I DIDN'T GET THAT SNOW-BLOWER FOR CHRISTMAS!

Calvin and HOBBES
by WATTERSON

WATTERSON

Calvin and Hobbes
by WATTERSON
WHOSE BRILLIANT IDEA WAS IT TO TAKE A HIKE OUT IN THIS BITTER COLD?! HOW MUCH LONGER DO WE HAVE TO DO THIS?

I FEEL LIKE I'M IN "DR. ZHIVAGO."
ALL RIGHT, CALVIN. YOU'VE MADE YOUR POINT, I THINK.

I HATE THESE FORCED MARCHES! WHEN ARE WE GOING HOME?
THIS IS JUST A LITTLE WALK, CALVIN. THE EXERCISE IS GOOD FOR YOU.

BUT I'M FREEZING! IT MUST BE 80 BELOW! MY TOES ARE NUMB!
NUMB TOES BUILD CHARACTER.

YEAH? WELL, WHAT ABOUT FROSTBITE?! WHAT ABOUT HYPOTHERMIA?! WHAT ABOUT DEATH?! I SUPPOSE THOSE BUILD CHARACTER TOO! I CANT BELIEVE I'M OUT HERE!

THIS IS THE WORST DAY OF MY ENTIRE LIFE! I HATE THIS! ARENT WE GOING HOME YET? IT SEEMS LIKE WE'VE BEEN WALKING FOR HOURS!
CALVIN, WILL YOU PLEASE STOP GRIPING?

GRIPING? I'M NOT GRIPING! I'M JUST OBSERVING WHAT A MISERABLE EXPERIENCE THIS IS! BUT OK! SURE! AS LONG AS I'M TRUDGING HUNDREDS OF MILES FOR NO APPARENT REASON, I MIGHT AS WELL DO IT IN SILENCE, RIGHT?!

JUST BECAUSE I'M OUT IN THE ELEMENTS LIKE A COMPLETE IDIOT, WATCHING MY DIGITS TURN TO ICE AND FALL OFF, I SURE AS HECK WOULDN'T EVER WANT TO SPOIL THE...
WE'RE HOME.

WE'RE WHAT? OH LOOK, WE'RE HOME!

WATTERSON

QUIZ:
Jack and Joe leave their homes at the same time and drive toward each other. Jack drives at 60 mph, while Joe drives at 30 mph. They pass each other in 10 minutes.

How far apart were Jack and Joe when they started?

IT WAS ANOTHER BAFFLING CASE. BUT THEN, YOU DON'T HIRE A PRIVATE EYE FOR THE EASY ONES...

I'D PLANNED TO TAKE THE DAY OFF AND SPEND TIME WITH A COUPLE OF BUDDIES. MY BUDDIES TRAVEL LIGHT AND THEY'RE FUN TO HAVE AROUND. ONE TRAVELS IN A HOLSTER, AND THE OTHER IN A HIP FLASK.
MY NAME IS BULLET. TRACER BULLET. WHAT PEOPLE CALL ME IS SOMETHING ELSE AGAIN. I'M A PRIVATE EYE. IT SAYS SO ON MY DOOR.
PRIVATE EYE

THE LAST THING I WANTED THIS MORNING WAS A CASE TO SOLVE, BUT THE DAME WHO BROUGHT IT WAS PERSUASIVE. MOST DAMES ARE, SOMEHOW.

GET TO WORK, CALVIN.
I TOLD HER IT WOULD COST HER FIFTY GREENBACKS A DAY, PLUS EXPENSES.

I STEPPED OUT INTO THE RAINY STREETS AND REVIEWED THE FACTS. THERE WEREN'T MANY.

TWO SAPS, JACK AND JOE, DRIVE TOWARD EACH OTHER AT 60 AND 30 MPH. AFTER 10 MINUTES, THEY PASS. I'M SUPPOSED TO FIND OUT HOW FAR APART THEY STARTED.

QUESTIONS POUR DOWN LIKE THE RAIN. WHO ARE THESE MUGS? WHAT WERE THEY TRYING TO ACCOMPLISH? WHY WAS JACK IN SUCH A HURRY? AND WHAT DIFFERENCE DOES IT MAKE WHERE THEY STARTED FROM??

I HAD A HUNCH THAT, BEFORE THIS WAS OVER, I'D BE SORRY I ASKED.

FIRST I FIGURED I'D TRY THE DERKINS DAME. SUSIE AND I NEVER HIT IT OFF, ALTHOUGH OCCASIONALLY WE HIT EACH OTHER.

SUSIE HAD A FACE THAT SUGGESTED SOMEBODY UPSTAIRS HAD A WEIRD SENSE OF HUMOR, BUT I WASN'T GOING TO HER PLACE FOR LAUGHS. I NEEDED INFORMATION.

THE WAY I LOOKED AT IT, DERKINS ACTED AWFULLY SMUG FOR A DAME WHO HAD A HEAD FOR NUMBERS AND NOT MUCH ELSE. MAYBE SHE'S GOT SOMETHING ON JACK AND JOE. THE QUESTION IS, WILL SHE SING?

NO, I WON'T TELL YOU WHAT THE ANSWER IS! DO YOUR OWN WORK!
WATTERSON

THE DERKINS DAME WASN'T TALKING. SOMEONE HAD GOTTEN TO HER FIRST AND SHUT HER UP GOOD. I KNEW SUSIE, AND CLOSING HER MOUTH WOULD'VE TAKEN SOME WORK.

I NEEDED A CLUE AND A DRINK. ONE OF THEM I KNEW WHERE TO FIND.

YOU'VE MADE ENOUGH TRIPS TO THE WATER FOUNTAIN. FINISH YOUR QUIZ.

SUDDENLY A GORILLA PULLED ME IN AN ALLEY, SQUEEZED MY SPINE INTO AN ACCORDION, AND PLAYED A POLKA ON ME WITH BRASS KNUCKLES!
YOUSE AIN'T GOIN' NOWHERE, FLATFOOT.
WATTERSON

THE INSIDE OF MY HEAD WAS EXPLODING WITH FIREWORKS. FORTUNATELY, MY LAST THOUGHT TURNED OUT THE LIGHTS WHEN IT LEFT.

WATTERSON

WHEN I CAME TO, THE PIECES ALL FIT TOGETHER. JACK AND JOE'S LIVES WERE DEFINED BY INTEGERS. OBVIOUSLY, THEY WERE PART OF A "NUMBERS" RACKET!

BACK IN THE OFFICE, I PULLED THE FILES ON ALL THE NUMBERS BIG ENOUGH TO KEEP SUSIE QUIET AND WANT ME OUT OF THE PICTURE. THE ANSWER HIT ME LIKE A .44 SLUG. IT HAD TO BE THE NUMBER THEY CALLED "MR. BILLION."

Answer: 1,000,000,000
TIME'S UP. BRING YOUR PAPERS FORWARD.
CASE CLOSED!
WHAT DID YOU GET, CALVIN? I THINK THE ANSWER'S 15.

Calvin and HOBBES
by WATTERSON

I THINK THIS IS MY FAVORITE TIME OF YEAR! THE NEW SNOW MAKES EVERYTHING LOOK SO PRETTY.

WUMPH!
WHOAAAAAA

I THINK THIS IS MY FAVORITE TIME OF YEAR! THE NEW SNOW MUFFLES APPROACHING FOOTSTEPS! HOO HOO!
MAN, I CAN'T WAIT FOR SPRING.
WATTERSON

Calvin and HOBBES
by WATTERSON
LET'S HURRY DOWN THIS HILL AND GO HOME.

WHAT'S THE RUSH?
THERE'S A TV SHOW ON SLEDDING I WANT TO WATCH.

IN MY OPINION, TELEVISION VALIDATES EXISTENCE.

TAKE THIS SLED RIDE, FOR INSTANCE. THE EXPERIENCE IS FLEETING AND ELUSIVE. BY TOMORROW, WE'LL HAVE FORGOTTEN IT, AND IT MAY AS WELL HAVE NOT EVEN HAPPENED.

BUT IF WE WERE ON TV NOW, COUNTLESS VIEWERS WOULD SHARE IN THE EVENT AND CONFIRM IT! THIS RIDE WOULD BECOME A PART OF MASS CONSCIOUSNESS!

AND ON TV, THE IMPACT OF AN EVENT IS DETERMINED BY THE IMAGE, NOT ITS SUBSTANCE.

SO WITH SOME STRONG VISUALS, OUR SLED RIDE COULD CONCEIVABLY MAKE US CULTURAL **ICONS**!

INSTEAD OF BEING BORING OL' CALVIN AND HOBBES, WE'D BE "CALVIN AND HOBBES-***AS SEEN ON TV***"! WOULDN'T THAT BE GREAT? DON'T YOU WISH WE WERE ON TV?

AT THIS MOMENT, I LIKE MY ANONYMITY.

I THINK WE SHOULD GO FOR THE HIGH-BROW PUBLIC TV AUDIENCE, DON'T YOU?
WATTERSON

I MISSED THE BUS, MOM.
OH NO.

HURRY! IF WE JUMP IN THE CAR, YOU CAN ZOOM UP, PASS THE BUS ON A STRAIGHTAWAY, DROP ME OFF AT A LATER STOP, AND I CAN RIDE THE BUS FROM THERE!

C'MON! WHAT ARE YOU WAITING FOR? REV UP THE CAR!

MOM'S SO LAZY.

READYYY... AIMMM....

BEDTIME, KIDDO.
AW, MOM! CAN'T I WATCH THE NEXT PROGRAM?

NO, YOU NEED YOUR SLEEP. C'MON.
CAN I JUST WATCH ANOTHER 15 MINUTES? PLEASE?? OK, JUST 10 MINUTES! THEN I'LL GO STRAIGHT TO BED! FIVE MINUTES! JUST FIVE MINUTES, OK?

TURN OFF THE TV.
LOOK, I'LL JUST WATCH A FEW MORE COMMERCIALS, OK? SEE, HERE'S MY FAVORITE GUM COMMERCIAL!

I GUESS THAT GOT PRETTY PATHETIC.

Calvin and Hobbes

by WATTERSON

OH NO! I JUST REMEMBERED THAT TODAY IS "SHOW AND TELL" DAY! I NEED SOMETHING TO SHOW AND TELL ABOUT!
CHOCOLATE FROSTED SUGAR BOMBS

WHY CAN'T YOU THINK OF THESE THINGS MORE THAN TWO MINUTES BEFORE THE BUS COMES?
WHAT CAN I TAKE? I'VE GOTTA TAKE SOMETHING!

I'VE.. AH...
ACHOOO

NEVER MIND, MOM! DO WE HAVE ANY PLASTIC BAGS?
I DON'T WANT TO KNOW. I DON'T WANT TO KNOW. I DON'T..

SEE? SEE? STARBOARD IS RIGHT! PORT IS LEFT!
OK, SO I WAS WRONG FOR ONCE IN MY LIFE! SHUT UP.

AARGHH! I MISSED! IT'S THESE DARN FUZZY MITTENS! THE SNOW STICKS TO 'EM AND YOU CAN'T THROW STRAIGHT! DARN IT! DARN IT! DARN IT!

I HATE THESE FUZZY MITTENS! IF ONLY MOM HAD GOTTEN ME PADDED GLOVES INSTEAD OF THESE NO-GOOD, AWFUL, ROTTEN FUZZY MITTENS!

WHAP!

WELL I'LL BE! MY FUZZY MITTENS HAVE PADS!

Calvin and Hobbes
by WATTERSON
THE INCREDIBLE SPACEMAN SPIFF, INTERPLANETARY EXPLORER EXTRAORDINAIRE, DESCENDS TOWARD AN ALIEN PLANET SURFACE!

ANOTHER DAY, ANOTHER MIND-BOGGLING ADVENTURE!

THE FEARLESS SPACEMAN SPIFF CRUISES LOW OVER PLANET QUORG, A DESOLATE WORLD OF DEEP GORGES AND CANYONS!

SEARCHING FOR LIFE, OUR HERO EXPLORES THE PECULIAR ROCK FORMATIONS!

...THE **VERY** PECULIAR ROCK FORMATIONS! ...A LITTLE **TOO** PECULIAR, PERHAPS!

SUDDENLY OUR HERO REALIZES THAT THIS LANDSCAPE WAS **NOT** CREATED BY **GEOLOGICAL** FORCES! SPIFF HITS THE THRUSTERS!

WHILE SPIFF WAS SEARCHING FOR ALIEN LIFE, IT SEEMS ALIEN LIFE WAS SEARCHING FOR SPIFF! NO DOUBT IT WANTED THE EARTHLING FOR DINNER!

CALVIN, WHERE ARE YOU?! IT'S TIME FOR DINNER!
UGHH! SPIFF BLASTS INTO HYPERSPACE!
WATTERSON

WUMP!

ANY DUMB KID CAN BUILD A SNOWMAN, BUT IT TAKES A GENIUS LIKE ME TO CREATE ART.

THIS SNOW SCULPTURE TRANSCENDS CORPOREAL LIKENESS TO EXPRESS DEEPER TRUTHS ABOUT THE HUMAN CONDITION! THIS SCULPTURE IS ABOUT GRIEF AND SUFFERING!

ONE LOOK AT THE TORTURED COUNTENANCE OF THIS FIGURE CONFIRMS THAT THE ARTIST HAS DRUNK DEEPLY FROM THE CUP OF LIFE! THIS WORK SHALL ENDURE AND INSPIRE FUTURE GENERATIONS!

STILL MAKING SNOW ART?
YEP!

YESTERDAY YOUR SCULPTURE MELTED.
THIS TIME I'M TAKING ADVANTAGE OF MY MEDIUM'S IMPERMANENCE.

THIS SCULPTURE IS ABOUT TRANSIENCE. AS THIS FIGURE MELTS, IT INVITES THE VIEWER TO CONTEMPLATE THE EVANESCENCE OF LIFE. THIS PIECE SPEAKS TO THE HORROR OF OUR OWN MORTALITY!

HEY STUPID! IT'S TOO WARM TO BUILD A SNOWMAN! WHAT A DOPE! HA HA HA HA!
A PHILISTINE ON THE SIDEWALK.
GENIUS IS NEVER UNDERSTOOD IN ITS OWN TIME.

HOW'S YOUR SNOW ART PROGRESSING?
I'VE MOVED INTO ABSTRACTION!

AH.
THIS PIECE IS ABOUT THE INADEQUACY OF TRADITIONAL IMAGERY AND SYMBOLS TO CONVEY MEANING IN TODAY'S WORLD.

BY ABANDONING REPRESENTATIONALISM, I'M FREE TO EXPRESS MYSELF WITH PURE FORM. SPECIFIC INTERPRETATION GIVES WAY TO A MORE VISCERAL RESPONSE.

I NOTICE YOUR OEUVRE IS MONOCHROMATIC.
WELL C'MON, IT'S JUST SNOW.

DAD, IF YOU THREW A SNOWBALL AT SOMEONE, BUT DELIBERATELY MISSED, WOULD THAT BE "BAD"?

WELL, I SUPPOSE THAT WOULD BE PROVOKING, SO YES, IT WOULD BE A LITTLE BAD.
AS BAD AS IF YOU'D HIT THE PERSON?

NO, NOT THAT BAD, BUT WORSE THAN IF YOU HADN'T THROWN IT AT ALL.
SUPPOSE YOU JUST GRAZED THE PERSON. HOW BAD WOULD THAT BE?

SAY MAYBE YOU KNOCKED OFF HIS HAT AND HIS GLASSES OR SOMETHING.
THAT WOULD MEAN INSTANT DEATH.

BOY, THIS PUDDING WAS GREAT! CAN I TAKE A BOWL UPSTAIRS TO HOBBES?
NO, I THINK YOU'VE HAD ENOUGH.

I DIDN'T SAY FOR ME. I SAID FOR HOBBES!
WELL, I DON'T THINK "HOBBES" NEEDS ANY EITHER.

WHY NOT?!
UM... BECAUSE TIGERS NEED TO STAY LEAN AND MEAN.

THAT'S WHAT SHE SAID.
I'M LEAN! I'M MEAN! TELL HER CHOCOLATE PUDDING MAKES MY COAT LUSTROUS.

Calvin and HOBBES
by WATTERSON

SSSSSS
SSSSSS

IF THERE'S MORE TO LIFE THAN THIS, I DON'T KNOW WHAT IT IS.
WATTERSON

WHY SHOULD I GO TO SCHOOL ?! WHY CAN'T I STAY HOME ?

WHY DO I HAVE TO LEARN ? WHY CAN'T I STAY THE WAY I AM? WHAT'S THE POINT OF THIS? WHY DO THINGS HAVE TO BE THIS WAY? WHY CAN'T THINGS BE DIFFERENT?

LIFE IS FULL OF MYSTERIES, ISN'T IT? SEE YOU THIS AFTERNOON.

AT 7:00 AM, MOM'S NOT VERY PHILOSOPHICAL.

ALL SET?
YEP!

OK, GET READY!

NOW!
CLICK
SMASH

TOO BAD THE BACK OF THE CAMERA OPENED WHEN WE LANDED. THAT WOULD'VE BEEN A GREAT PICTURE!

HA! I'VE GOT A GREAT WORD AND IT'S ON A "DOUBLE WORD SCORE" BOX!

"ZQFMGB" ISN'T A WORD! IT DOESN'T EVEN HAVE A VOWEL!
IT IS **SO** A WORD! IT'S A WORM FOUND IN NEW GUINEA! EVERYONE KNOWS THAT!

I'M LOOKING IT UP.
YOU DO, AND I'LL LOOK UP THAT 12-LETTER WORD ***YOU*** PLAYED WITH ALL THE Xs AND Js!

WHAT'S YOUR SCORE FOR ZQFMGB?
957.

HEY, NO TV UNTIL YOUR HOMEWORK IS DONE.
IT'S GETTING DONE.

NOT WITH YOU SITTING **HERE**, IT ISN'T.
HOBBES IS READING MY BOOK FOR ME.

AFTER I'M DONE WATCHING TV, HE'LL TELL **ME** WHAT THE BOOK WAS ABOUT, AND I'LL TELL **HIM** WHAT THE TV SHOWS WERE ABOUT! SEE, WE'RE DOING TWICE AS MUCH IN THE SAME AMOUNT OF TIME!

MOM SAYS **YOU** SHOULD WATCH TV AND **I** SHOULD READ THE DUMB BOOK.
UGH, I ONLY LIKE NATURE DOCUMENTARIES.

Hey Twinky, gimme a quarter.

WHAT?! WHY SHOULD I GIVE YOU MY MONEY?!

It's for the "Let Calvin Live Through Recess Fund."
SOUNDS LIKE A WORTHY CAUSE.

HIS MOTTO IS "GIVE BEFORE IT HURTS."

MOMMM! I NEED A DRINK OF WATER!

MPHHH... CALVIN, IT'S AFTER MIDNIGHT. GET A DRINK YOURSELF.
I CAN'T. THERE ARE MONSTERS UNDER MY BED! I'M SCARED.

OK... OK... OK...

AAUGH

Calvin and Hobbes
by WATTERSON

140 MILLION YEARS AGO, THE INCREDIBLE 'ULTRASAURS' WANDER THE EARTH! SOME WEIGH OVER 70 TONS, AND EVEN THE VICIOUS ALLOSAURS ARE NO MATCH FOR THESE GIANTS!

BUT WAIT! A DISTANT RUMBLING SENDS THE ULTRASAURS INTO A PANICKED STAMPEDE! IS IT A VOLCANO? IS IT AN EARTHQUAKE?

NO! IT'S.. IT'S A **CALVINOSAURUS**!

NAMED AFTER THE RENOWNED ARCHEOLOGIST WHO DISCOVERED IT, THE HUGE CALVINOSAUR CAN EAT AN ULTRASAUR IN A SINGLE BITE!

PHOOEY! I NEVER FIND ***ANY***THING.
IT LOOKS LIKE YOU'VE HIT THE SEWER PIPE.
WATTERSON

OK HOBBES, TOSS UP THIS DECK OF CARDS, AND I'LL PLUG THE ACE OF SPADES!
OH BOY, A SHOOTING TRICK!

GO!
BLAM
BAM
POW
ZING
BLOOIE
BANG

HERE IT IS! WOW! SIX CLEAN HOLES THROUGH THE ACE!
PRETTY GOOD, HUH? WANT TO KNOW HOW I DID IT? I USED A HOLE PUNCHER AHEAD OF TIME!

HMM, ON SECOND THOUGHT, I'LL FOLD.
HEY, WHAT'S WITH THIS DECK?!

THIS MORNING I HAD A WONDERFUL DREAM. BY HOLDING MY ARMS OUT STIFF AND PUSHING DOWN HARD, I FOUND I COULD SUSPEND MYSELF A FEW FEET ABOVE THE GROUND. I FLAPPED HARDER, AND SOON I WAS SOARING EFFORTLESSLY OVER THE TREES AND TELEPHONE POLES! I COULD FLY! I FOLDED MY ARMS BACK AND ZOOMED LOW OVER THE NEIGHBORHOOD. EVERYONE WAS AMAZED, AND THEY RAN ALONG UNDER ME AS I SHOT BY. THEN I ROCKETED UP SO FAST THAT MY EYES WATERED FROM THE WIND. I LAUGHED AND LAUGHED, MAKING HUGE LOOPS ACROSS THE SKY! ...THAT'S WHEN MOM WOKE ME UP AND SAID I WAS GOING TO MISS THE BUS IF I DIDN'T GET MY BOTTOM OUT OF BED; 20 MINUTES LATER, HERE I AM, STANDING IN THE COLD RAIN, WAITING TO GO TO SCHOOL, AND I JUST REMEMBERED I FORGOT MY LUNCH.

TUESDAYS DON'T START MUCH WORSE THAN THIS.

I DID IT! I DID IT!

SOMEHOW I IMAGINED THIS EXPERIENCE WOULD BE MORE REWARDING.

HEWWO! IS HOBBESIE-WOBBSIE SWEEPY? OOH, HE'S JUST A BIG SNOOGIE-WOOGIE, ISN'T HE? YES HE *IS!* HEWWO, SNOOGIE-WOOGIE!

GLOMP!
HEY! HEY!

OW! LEGGO, YOU BLOODTHIRSTY CARNIVORE!
OW!
OW!
OW!

I CAN SEE WHY LITTLE TABBY CATS ARE SO MUCH MORE POPULAR.

ONCE UPON A TIME, THERE WAS A...
HOLD IT.

YOU KNOW WHAT *I'D* LIKE TO SEE? I'D LIKE TO SEE THE THREE BEARS EAT THE THREE LITTLE PIGS, AND THEN THE BEARS JOIN UP WITH THE BIG BAD WOLF AND EAT GOLDILOCKS AND LITTLE RED RIDING HOOD!

TELL ME A STORY LIKE *THAT*, OK?

AND HOW SHOULD HANSEL AND GRETEL MEET *THEIR* UNTIMELY DEMISE?
THE WITCH EATS THEM AND THEN THE WOLF EATS THE WITCH.

HEY DAD, CAN I TAKE THE GAS CAN FOR THE LAWN MOWER OUT IN THE BACK YARD?

WHAT ON EARTH FOR? IT'S 8:00 AT NIGHT!
I WANT TO POUR GASOLINE IN BIG LETTERS ON THE LAWN...

.. AND SET FIRE TO IT SO AIRPLANES CAN READ IT AS THEY FLY OVER!
NO, YOU CAN'T DO THAT! DON'T BE RIDICULOUS!

I DONT EVEN WANT TO KNOW WHAT HE INTENDED TO WRITE.

Calvin and HOBBES
by WATTERSON
BEWARE! FALLING BUCKEYES

HERE COMES SOMEBODY!

THIS MEETING OF THE TOP SECRET CLUB G.R.O.S.S. (GET RID OF SLIMY GIRLS) WILL COME TO ORDER. TODAY THIS AUGUST ASSEMBLY WILL DECIDE WHETHER TO DEMOTE PRESIDENT HOBBES ON CHARGES OF HERESY!

HERESY?!

LET THE RECORD SHOW THAT THE DEFENDANT MADE AN UNDISPARAGING COMMENT ABOUT THE POSSIBLE MEMBERSHIP OF SUSIE DERKINS, AN ADMITTED GIRL AND ENEMY OF THIS CLUB.

LET THE RECORD ALSO SHOW THAT SUPREME DICTATOR-FOR-LIFE CALVIN IS A NINCOMPOOP.
OK, JUST FOR THAT, YOU'RE ALSO CHARGED WITH INSUBORDINATION! THIS COURT FINDS YOU GUILTY ON BOTH COUNTS AND STRIPS YOU OF YOUR TITLE!

HA! AS COURT STENOGRAPHER, I REFUSE TO ENTER THE VERDICT! IN FACT, I'M PROMOTING MYSELF TO "EL TIGRE NUMERO UNO"!
OH YEAH?! WELL THEN, I PROMOTE MYSELF TO "MOST HIGHEST, GRANDEST, EXALTED, UM, SUPREME, UH..

THERE! I WROTE "HOBBES EQUALS GREAT" IN THE OFFICIAL CLUB NOTEBOOK! NOW IT'S A LAW!
IT IS NOT! GIMME THAT!
HOBS = GRAT
WATTERSON

HA HA HA! I'M WRITING "HOBBES EQUALS UGLY FUR BALL"! WHAT DO YOU THINK OF THAT?
OH HO! I TAKE THE SUPREME DICTATOR HAT! NOW I'M THE SUPREME DICTATOR!

YOU GIVE THAT BACK!
I DECLARE YOU NULL AND VOID!

TRUCE?
TRUCE.

WHAT A GREAT CLUB. TOO BAD WE DON'T HAVE MORE MEMBERS.
MAYBE WE SHOULD ALLOW SUSIE TO JOIN.

DO YOU... I MEAN, DOES **HOBBES** WANT ANY TUNA FISH THIS WEEK?

NO, HOBBES STOPPED EATING CANNED TUNA. YOU KNOW, THEY KILL DOLPHINS TO GET IT.
OK, I'LL PUT IT BACK.

SO WHAT DOES HOBBES LIKE NOW INSTEAD?

FRESH SWORDFISH STEAKS. HE LIKES THEM GRILLED OUTSIDE.
MM-HMM. HOW ABOUT PEANUT BUTTER?

HERE'S SOME CLEAN CLOTHES. WILL YOU PUT THEM AWAY PLEASE?

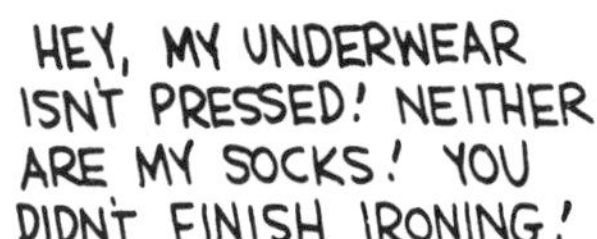
HEY, MY UNDERWEAR ISN'T PRESSED! NEITHER ARE MY SOCKS! YOU DIDN'T FINISH IRONING!

BUDDY, IF YOU WANT YOUR UNDERWEAR IRONED, YOU CAN DO IT YOURSELF!
WHAT KIND OF MOTHER **ARE** YOU?!

SHE SHOULD TAKE MORE PRIDE IN HER WORK.

I ASKED MOM IF I WAS A GIFTED CHILD. ...SHE SAID THEY CERTAINLY WOULDN'T HAVE **PAID** FOR ME.

YOU CAN RELATE THIS LITTLE STORY WHEN THE REPORTERS ASK HOW I WENT BAD.

MOM! HOBBES IS READING MY COMIC BOOKS! TELL HIM TO STOP!

I TOLD HIM TO GO BUY HIS OWN, AND HE **SNARLED** AT ME! MAKE HIM GIVE 'EM BACK!
MAYBE YOU SHOULD BE GLAD HE'S MORE LITERATE THAN MOST STUFFED ANIMALS.

BUT THEY'RE **MY** COMIC BOOKS, NOT **HIS**!
WELL, YOU SHOULD LEARN TO SHARE. I DON'T THINK HOBBES WILL HURT THEM.

ARE YOU KIDDING?! HE DREW A MUSTACHE AND GLASSES ON EVERY PICTURE OF NUKE-MAN LAST ISSUE! IN **PEN**!
WHY DON'T YOU GO PLAY OUTSIDE, CALVIN.

HOW'S YOUR MATH COMING?

I DON'T **DO** MATH ANY MORE. I DECIDED I'M MORE OF A "VISUAL" PERSON.

GOOD. VISUALIZE BEING THE ONLY 45-YEAR-OLD IN FIRST GRADE.

VISUALIZING A FEW SUMS NOW, EH?
ACTUALLY, I'M VISUALIZING **YOU** IN TRACTION. HELP ME DO THESE, OK?

HEY HOBBES, I'LL GIVE YOU 20 QUESTIONS TO GUESS WHAT I HAVE IN MY HANDS, OK?
OK. IS IT LOATHSOME?
YES!
IS IT SOME BIG CENTIPEDE WITH POISON PINCHERS?
CENTIPEDES HAVE POISON PINCHERS?
I THINK SO.
MAN, IT'S A GOOD THING YOU GUESSED IT SO FAST!
WITH YOU, IT'S NEVER TOO DIFFICULT.

Calvin and HOBBES

by WATTERSON

Z

NYUP NYUP

WHERE DO WE KEEP THE EXTENSION CORDS?
IN THE PANTRY, ON THE BOTTOM SHELF.

WHERE DO WE KEEP THE BLADES FOR DAD'S ELECTRIC SAW?
IN THE... WHY DO YOU WANT TO KNOW?

HUH? OH, I'M JUST MAKING AN INVENTORY LIST SO WE'LL ALWAYS KNOW WHERE TO FIND THINGS.

I GET THE FEELING THERE WAS NO RIGHT ANSWER TO THAT QUESTION.

CALVIN, COME OUT FROM WHEREVER YOU'RE HIDING AND TAKE YOUR BATH!

DO YOU HEAR ME, CALVIN?! I MEAN NOW!

OH NO! LOOK AT YOU! AUGH! GET OFF THE RUG!

LIKE IT'S MY FAULT SHE HASN'T GOTTEN THE CHIMNEY SWEPT.

MOM! MOM! I JUST SAW THE FIRST ROBIN OF SPRING! CALL THE NEWSPAPER QUICK!

HA HA! A FRONT PAGE WRITE-UP! A COMMEMORATIVE PLAQUE! A CIVIC CEREMONY! ALL FOR ME! HOORAY! HOORAY!
OH BOY! SHOULD I PUT THE PRIZE MONEY IN A TRUST FUND, OR BLOW IT ALL AT ONCE? HA HA! I CAN'T BELIEVE I DID IT!
CALVIN...

IT'S A HARD, BITTER, CRUEL WORLD TO HAVE TO GROW UP IN, HOBBES.
CHEER UP! DID I TELL YOU I SAW A ROBIN YESTERDAY?

I SURE LIKE CHOCOLATE FROSTED SUGAR BOMBS! LOOK HOW BROWN THE MILK GETS!
UGH.

WANT TO SEE SOMETHING WEIRD? LOOK AT THE NUTRITIONAL INFORMATION ON THE BACK PANEL.

WOW. 100% OF THE DAILY RECOMMENDED ALLOWANCE OF CAFFEINE!
HEY LOOK! YOU CAN SEND AWAY FOR A CHOCOLATE FROSTED SUGAR BOMBS "BUZZY THE HUMMINGBIRD" DOLL!

EENIE, MEENIE, MINEY, MOE! CATCH A TIGER BY THE TOE!
!

IF HE HOLLERS, UM... UH... ..HEH HEH...

WHO WRITES THESE DUMB THINGS ANYWAY?

COUNTY LIBRARY? YES, DO YOU HAVE ANY BOOKS ON HOMEMADE BOMBS?

THAT'S WHAT I SAID. I NEED A BOOK THAT LISTS SUPPLIES AND GIVES STEP-BY-STEP INSTRUCTIONS FOR BUILDING, RIGGING, AND DETONATING THEM.

WELL WHAT ABOUT YOUR OTHER BRANCHES? DON'T *THEY* HAVE ANY BOOKS LIKE THAT?

BOY, AND PEOPLE WONDER WHY KIDS DON'T READ.

Calvin and HobbEs

by WATTERSON

I'M FREE! I'M FREE!

AT LAST! HOME SWEET HO...

OH NO.

HOO HOO! THAT WAS A GOOD ONE! LOOK HOW FAR WE LANDED!
A HOUSE WITH A TIGER IS NEVER A HOME.

LOOK AT YOU! HOW COULD ANYONE GET SO DIRTY AT SCHOOL?
I GOT THIS DIRTY JUST TRYING TO WALK IN THE FRONT DOOR! OL' CATAPULT BUTT WAS LYING IN WAIT FOR ME.

WELL, IT DOESN'T MATTER. YOU'D BETTER GET IN THE TUB NOW ANYWAY.
A BATH?!
BUT IT'S THE MIDDLE OF THE AFTERNOON!

YES, BUT I HAVE TO GET IN THE SHOWER BEFORE YOUR DAD GETS HOME, SO HE CAN TAKE ONE.
WHY ALL THE BATHS? IS THERE SOME EPIDEMIC GOING AROUND?

I TOLD YOU THIS MORNING WE'RE GOING OUT TONIGHT. ROSALYN WILL BE HERE AT 6:00.
AUGHHHH!

AAAAUUUUUUUUUGGGGGGGHHHHHHHHHHH!
LOOK, I KNOW YOU DON'T LIKE ROSALYN, BUT SHE'S THE ONLY BABY SITTER I COULD GET.
AND YOU REMEMBER OUR TALK AFTER WHAT HAPPENED LAST TIME, DON'T YOU? I WANT YOU ON YOUR BEST BEHAVIOR TONIGHT.
YOU DO EXACTLY WHAT SHE TELLS YOU. I DON'T WANT TO COME HOME AND HEAR ANY HORROR STORIES, OK?
FOR GOODNESS SAKE, CALVIN! TAKE A BREATH BEFORE YOU PASS OUT ON THE FLOOR!

WHAT ARE WE GOING TO DO, HOBBES? ROSALYN WILL BE HERE IN JUST A FEW HOURS!
DO YOU THINK SHE'LL REMEMBER HOW YOU LOCKED HER OUTSIDE LAST TIME?

IF SHE DOES, WE'RE DEAD! SHE'LL PROBABLY STICK MY HEAD ON A STAKE IN THE FRONT YARD AS A WARNING TO OTHER KIDS SHE BABY-SITS!
I'M ALMOST SURE THAT WOULD VIOLATE SOME ZONING ORDINANCE.

WELL NO MATTER WHAT, WE'RE IN BIG TROUBLE UNLESS WE THINK OF SOMETHING FAST!
I SUPPOSE WE COULD TRY BEING GOOD.

I MUST'VE GOTTEN WATER IN MY EAR. WHAT DID YOU SAY?
NOTHING. FORGET IT.

HI ROSALYN, COME ON IN. THANKS FOR COMING AGAIN.
NO TROUBLE.

HI ROSALYN! YOU DON'T NEED TO WORRY THIS TIME. CALVIN WILL BE ON HIS BEST BEHAVIOR TONIGHT.
EVEN SO, I'D LIKE AN ADVANCE.

AN ADVANCE? BUT... BUT...
DEAR, MAY I SPEAK WITH YOU A MOMENT?

BUT WE GAVE HER AN ADVANCE ON TONIGHT WHEN SHE LEFT LAST TIME!
I DON'T CARE. JUST PAY WHAT IT TAKES TO GET US OUT OF HERE!

OK, WE'RE GOING. ...AND CALVIN?
YES?

GCKKHHK!

I THINK I'LL SIT IN THE MIDDLE OF THE FLOOR AND LOOK AT THE WALL TONIGHT.
GOOD. I'LL TELL YOU WHEN IT'S BEDTIME.

THIS IS AWFUL! IF WE STEP OUT OF LINE ONCE TONIGHT, ROSALYN WILL KILL US, AND THEN MOM AND DAD WILL KILL US AGAIN WHEN THEY GET HOME.

I GUESS THAT'S THAT.
WHAT?! ADMIT DEFEAT? NEVER!

THINGS MAY LOOK GRIM FOR US, BUT NOTHING IS GRIM FOR...

...STUPENDOUS MAN! CHAMPION OF LIBERTY! FOE OF TYRANNY!
I'M GOING TO GET IN BED NOW AND AVOID THE RUSH.

A BOLT OF FIERY CRIMSON STREAKS ACROSS THE SKY! IT'S STUPENDOUS MAN!

THE FIENDISH BABY SITTER GIRL HAS A LOCAL HOUSEHOLD IN HER IRON GRIP OF TERROR! THE MAN OF MEGA-MIGHT ZOOMS TO THE RESCUE!

I'M IN LUCK! BABY SITTER GIRL IS MOMENTARILY DISTRACTED!

HI CHARLIE, IT'S ROSALYN. YEAH, I'M OVER AT THE LITTLE MONSTER'S HOUSE AGAIN. HMM? NO, ACTUALLY HE'S BEEN PRETTY GOOD TONIGHT. YEAH, I CAN'T BELIEVE IT.

ANYWAY CHARLIE, I'M SORRY WE COULDN'T GO OUT TONIGHT, BUT THIS LITTLE CREEP'S PARENTS ARE SO DESPERATE TO GET AWAY FROM HIM ONCE IN A WHILE THAT THEY...

YAHH! FREEDOM AND JUSTICE SHALL ALWAYS PREVAIL OVER TYRANNY, BABY SITTER GIRL!
!?!

GET OFF ME, CALVIN, YOU PEST! OW! LET GO! QUIT IT!
STUPENDOUS MAN HAS THE STRENGTH OF A MILLION MORTAL MEN! GIVE UP!

LISTEN CHARLIE, I'M GOING TO HAVE TO CALL YOU BACK. YOU WOULDN'T BELIEVE WHAT THIS CRETIN IS WEARING.
WITH MUSCLES OF MAGNITUDE, STUPENDOUS MAN FIGHTS WITH HEROIC RESOLVE!

SEE, IF WE HAD BOUGHT A DOG INSTEAD, LIKE I WANTED, WE COULD GO OUT LIKE THIS ALL THE TIME.
HONEY, WE CAME HERE TO RELAX. LET'S TALK ABOUT SOMETHING ELSE.

THERE GOES ROSALYN AROUND THE HOUSE AGAIN. SHE STILL DOESN'T KNOW YOU SNEAKED BACK INSIDE.
NOW I'LL CHANGE BACK INTO MY SECRET IDENTITY ALTER EGO!

UH OH. SHE SAW THE LIGHT ON IN THIS ROOM. SHE'S COMING IN!
QUICK! GET IN THE COVERS! PRETEND WE'VE JUST BEEN READING IN BED!

BUT SHE KNOWS YOU ATTACKED HER AND RAN OUTSIDE HALF AN HOUR AGO!
THAT WAS STUPENDOUS MAN, NOT MILD-MANNERED CALVIN! I'VE BEEN IN BED WITH MY PJs ON SINCE 8:00.

YOU THINK SHE'S GOING TO BELIEVE THAT?
MY COVERS ARE HERE. MY PAJAMAS ARE HERE. IT'S AS PLAIN AS CAN BE!

ALL RIGHT! I FOUND YOU!
FOUND?? WHY, WHAT DO YOU MEAN? I'VE BEEN IN BED READING ALL EVENING WITH HOBBES.

DON'T GIVE ME THAT! YOU JUST NOW SNEAKED INSIDE, TOOK OFF YOUR SILLY COSTUME, AND JUMPED IN BED! I KNOW WHAT YOU DID! WELL YOU'RE GONNA GET IT NOW, BUCKO!

OH YEAH? WHAT ARE YOU GOING TO DO TO ME, HUH? YOU CANT SEND ME TO BED WHEN I'M ALREADY IN BED! SORRY TO SPOIL YOUR FUN, YOU EEL!

OK, DOWNSTAIRS! MARCH!
HEY, YOU CAN'T TAKE ME OUT OF BED! I NEED MY SLEEP! HEY! HEY!

WHILE YOUR DAD IS TAKING ROSALYN HOME, PERHAPS YOU'D LIKE TO EXPLAIN WHAT HAPPENED TONIGHT.

GOSH MOM, WHAT'S TO TELL? AT 8:00, I PUT ON MY PAJAMAS, BRUSHED MY TEETH AND WENT STRAIGHT TO BED. NOTHING HAPPENED.

AND THIS?
UH... LIES! ALL LIES! ROSALYN MADE ME DO THAT JUST SO I'D GET IN TROUBLE! SHE HATES KIDS! NONE OF THAT IS TRUE! I WENT STRAIGHT TO BED!

NICE TRY, PINOCCHIO.
WELL WHO WOUD'VE THOUGHT ROSALYN WOULD MAKE ME WRITE A FULL CONFESSION ?!

Calvin and HOBBES by WATTERSON

LIFE'S DISAPPOINTMENTS ARE HARDER TO TAKE WHEN YOU DON'T KNOW ANY SWEAR WORDS.

BOY, I'M IN A ROTTEN MOOD. THE WORLD HAD JUST BETTER LOOK OUT!

HEY YOU, YOU'RE IN MY WAY! MOVE IT!

WHAT'S THE MATTER? DID YOU GO DEAF?! GET OUT OF MY WAY! SCRAM!

C'MON, HURRY UP! YOU THINK I'VE GOT ALL DAY?!

NOW ARE YOU GOING TO STEP ASIDE, OR *WHAT*?! I'M COMING THROUGH!

MMPH! GGGHH! WHAT ARE YOU DOING?! I *SAID* MOVE ASIDE!!

DOGGONE IT, WHEN I SAY *MOVE*, I EXPECT YOU TO JUMP! *MOVE*!

MOVE! MOVE! MOVE! MOVE! MOVE!

HEY! PUT ME DOWN! WHERE ARE YOU TAKING ME?! I DEMAND AN EXPLANA... HEY, IS THAT A MUD HOLE?! YOU'D BETTER NOT! YOU HEAR ME?!

SEE WHY I'M IN SUCH A BAD MOOD?!?

NO TV FOR A WEEK! WHAT INJUSTICE!

THEY THINK THEY'VE WON, BUT THEY HAVEN'T!

I'LL SHOW 'EM! I REFUSE TO LEARN A LESSON!

I'M INDOMITABLE! THEY CAN'T CHANGE ME!

I'LL SIT IN FRONT OF THE TV ALL WEEK EVEN IF I CAN'T TURN IT ON!

DAD, WILL YOU EXPLAIN THE THEORY OF RELATIVITY TO ME? I DON'T UNDERSTAND WHY TIME GOES SLOWER AT GREAT SPEED.

IT'S BECAUSE YOU KEEP CHANGING TIME ZONES. SEE, IF YOU FLY TO CALIFORNIA, YOU GAIN THREE HOURS ON A FIVE-HOUR FLIGHT, RIGHT?

SO IF YOU GO AT THE SPEED OF LIGHT, YOU GAIN MORE TIME, BECAUSE IT DOESN'T TAKE AS LONG TO GET THERE. OF COURSE, THE THEORY OF RELATIVITY ONLY WORKS IF YOU'RE GOING WEST.

GEE, THAT'S NOT WHAT MOM SAID AT ALL! SHE MUST BE TOTALLY OFF HER ROCKER.
WELL, WE MEN ARE BETTER AT ABSTRACT REASONING. GO TELL HER THAT.

MOM, CAN WE GO OUT TO THE HIGHWAY?
DO WHAT?

SEE, I'LL PUT ON MY ROLLER SKATES AND TIE A ROPE FROM THE CAR BUMPER TO MY WAIST. THEN WHEN I GIVE YOU THE HIGH FIVE, YOU PATCH OUT WHILE I RIDE BEHIND AT 55 MPH!

WHAT DO YOU SAY? CAN WE GO?

I SURE WISH YOU COULD DRIVE.

Calvin and HOBBES
by WATTERSON
ACE PILOT SPACEMAN SPIFF CRUISES LOW OVER THE PLANET AT HIGH SPEED!

I WONDER WHAT THIS "E" ON THE FUEL GAUGE MEANS.

THE INTREPID SPACEMAN SPIFF LANDS ON PLANET GORZARG-5!

OUR HERO SETS OFF ACROSS THE DESOLATE TERRAIN IN SEARCH OF HELP! IN THE DISTANCE, METHANE CLOUDS RAIN SODIUM HYDROXIDE, A CAUSTIC ALKALI!

OH NO! THE DOWNPOUR WAS TOO HEAVY FOR THE GROUND TO ABSORB! A STEAMING RIVER OF CORROSIVE LIQUID RUSHES TOWARD OUR HERO!

THE BRAVE SPACEMAN SPIFF SCRAMBLES TO HIGHER GROUND, BUT THE FLOOD CONTINUES TO RISE!

OUR HERO IS TRAPPED! IT'S ONLY A MATTER OF TIME UNTIL THE FOAMING, NOXIOUS WASH CLEANS THE MEAT FROM SPIFF'S BONES! HOW COULD THINGS EVER GET WORSE?!
WATTERSON

AUGHH! AN ALIEN COMES TO PUSH HIM IN!
FOR HEAVEN'S SAKE, CALVIN! JUST GET IN!

WOW! NOBODY IS ON THE SWINGS! I CAN'T BELIEVE IT!

HA HA! I ALMOST *NEVER* GET A SWING AT RECESS!
THIS IS GREAT!
NO ONE IS TELLING ME TO HURRY UP!
HIGHER! HIGHER!
WHEE!

..EITHER THIS IS MY LUCKY DAY, OR I MISSED THE END-OF-RECESS BELL AGAIN.

HEY CALVIN, DIDN'T YOU SIGN UP TO PLAY BASEBALL AT RECESS?
NO, WHY?

YOU MUST BE THE ONLY BOY WHO DIDN'T. ALL THE OTHERS ARE PLAYING IN THE BACK FIELDS.
YOU MEAN I'M THE ONLY BOY ON A PLAYGROUND FULL OF *GIRLS?!*

IT SURE LOOKS LIKE IT. WANT TO RIDE ON THE TEETER-TOTTER WITH ME?
OH NO! I'M IN *COOTIE CENTRAL!* I HAVEN'T HAD MY SHOTS!

RELAX. STUPIDITY PRODUCES ANTIBODIES.
AIR FILTER! AIR FILTER!

WHY DIDN'T YOU SIGN UP TO PLAY BASE-BALL LIKE THE REST OF THE BOYS? DON'T YOU LIKE SPORTS?
I DUNNO. I'D JUST RATHER RUN AROUND.

I HATE ALL THE RULES AND ORGANIZATION AND TEAMS AND RANKS IN SPORTS.

SOMEBODY'S ALWAYS YELLING AT YOU, TELLING YOU WHERE TO BE, WHAT TO DO, AND WHEN TO DO IT.

I FIGURE WHEN I WANT *THAT*, I'LL JOIN THE ARMY AND AT LEAST GET PAID.

WELL, SPORTS ARE GOOD FOR YOU. THEY TEACH TEAMWORK AND COOPERATION. YOU LEARN HOW TO WIN GRACIOUSLY AND ACCEPT DEFEAT. IT BUILDS CHARACTER.

EVERY TIME I'VE BUILT CHARACTER, I'VE REGRETTED IT! I DON'T WANT TO LEARN TEAMWORK! I DON'T WANT TO LEARN ABOUT WINNING AND LOSING! HECK, I DON'T EVEN WANT TO COMPETE! WHAT'S WRONG WITH JUST HAVING FUN BY YOURSELF, HUH?!

C'MON, LET'S GO OUTSIDE AND TRY SOME CATCHES BEFORE DINNER, OK? A LITTLE PRACTICE WILL MAKE YOU MORE CONFIDENT TOMORROW AT RECESS.
I HATE THESE FATHER-SON THINGS.

GO OUT A LITTLE BIT, AND I'LL HIT YOU A GROUNDER.
WHY DID I SIGN UP FOR THIS? I SHOULD JUST MOVE.

READY? NOW, BE SURE TO RUN UP TO THE BALL. DON'T JUST LET IT ROLL TO YOU.

ARE YOU OK? SOMETIMES THE BALL BOUNCES UP LIKE THAT, AND YOU'VE GOT TO BE READY.
THAGS FOR THE TIB, DAD. FIDE MY NODE AND PUD ID IN ICE SO THEY CAN SEW ID BAG OD!

GOODNESS, WHAT HAPPENED?! YOU WERE ONLY OUT THERE A MINUTE!
A GROUNDER BOUNCED UP AND HIT CALVIN IN THE NOSE.

I'B BLEEDIG! BY ODE DAD ID TRYIG TO GILL ME!
HOLD YOUR HEAD BACK, HONEY. HERE'S SOME MORE TISSUES.

I'B NOD PLAYIG BADEBALL EDDY MORE! NEBBER AGAIN! I HADE IT!
SIT STILL SO THE BLEEDING CAN STOP, OK?

I GUESS WE CAN FORGET HAVING A MILLIONAIRE BASEBALL PLAYER SUPPORT US IN OUR OLD AGE.
DEAR!
ALL BY CHARAGDER ID DRIPPIG OUT BY NODE!

HOW'S THE NOSE?
IT FINALLY STOPPED BLEEDING. I GUESS THAT MEANS I'LL HAVE TO GO TO SCHOOL TOMORROW.

MY WHOLE LIFE IS A DISASTER. I GET INJURED JUST TRYING TO LEARN THE SKILLS IT TAKES TO PLAY A GAME I DON'T EVEN WANT TO PLAY!

YOUR NOSE IS PROBABLY ALL CLOGGED UP NOW, HUH?
SNRKK YEAH, WHY?

IF YOU SNORE, I'M TILTING THE BED SO YOU ROLL OUT THE WINDOW.
IT'S ALWAYS NICE TO HAVE A SYMPATHETIC FRIEND TO TALK TO.

I SEE YOU'RE BRINGING A GLOVE TODAY. DID YOU SIGN UP FOR RECESS BASEBALL?
YEAH, DON'T REMIND ME.

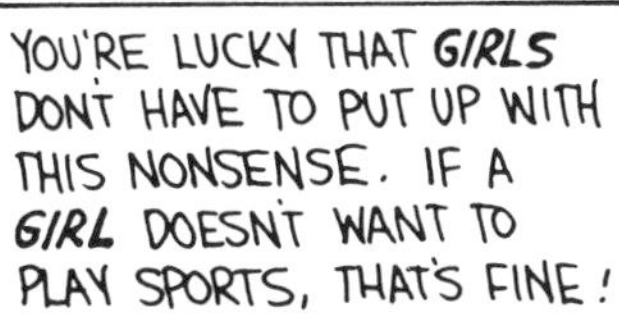
YOU'RE LUCKY THAT **GIRLS** DON'T HAVE TO PUT UP WITH THIS NONSENSE. IF A **GIRL** DOESN'T WANT TO PLAY SPORTS, THAT'S FINE!

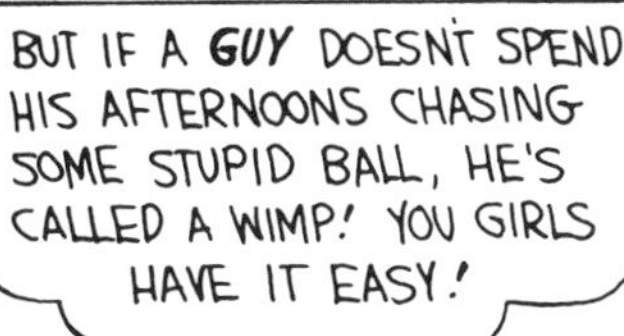
BUT IF A **GUY** DOESN'T SPEND HIS AFTERNOONS CHASING SOME STUPID BALL, HE'S CALLED A WIMP! YOU GIRLS HAVE IT EASY!

ON THE OTHER HAND, **BOYS** AREN'T EXPECTED TO SPEND THEIR LIVES 20 POUNDS UNDERWEIGHT.
AND IF YOU DON'T PLAY SPORTS, YOU DON'T GET TO MAKE BEER COMMERCIALS!

MR. LOCKJAW? I'M CALVIN. I'M SUPPOSED TO BE ON TEAM FIVE NOW.
OH YES, YOU'RE THE ONE WHO SIGNED UP LATE. HMM... OK, YOU GO PLAY LEFT FIELD.

LEFT FIELD. OK, I KNOW THAT. LET'S SEE, IF I'M **HERE**, THEN LEFT FIELD WOULD BE...
THAT WAY. PLAY **DEEP** LEFT FIELD.

I GUESS THIS IS PRETTY DEEP.

I THINK BASEBALL IS THE MOST BORING GAME IN THE WORLD. I'VE BEEN STANDING OUT HERE IN DEEP LEFT FIELD ALL THIS TIME, AND NOT A SINGLE BALL HAS COME OUT HERE!

ACTUALLY, I SUPPOSE THAT'S JUST AS WELL. I DON'T KNOW WHAT BASE TO THROW TO ANYWAY. IN FACT, I'M NOT EVEN SURE I CAN THROW THAT FAR.

HEY, WHAT'S EVERYONE DOING? ARE PEOPLE SWITCHING TEAMS, OR WHAT? THE GUYS AT BAT ARE NOW OUT **HERE**!

WELL, I'M SURE SOMEONE WOULD TELL ME IF I WAS SUPPOSED TO BE DOING ANYTHING DIFFERENT.

OUR HERO, THE FEARLESS SPACEMAN SPIFF, IS MAROONED ON THE MOST DISTANT PLANET IN THE GALAXY!

THERE'S NO HOPE OF RESCUE FROM THIS BLEAK AND ISOLATED WORLD!

OH, WHAT A DESOLATE PLACE TO BE TRAPPED! SPIFF TRIES DESPERATELY TO REPAIR HIS DISABLED SPACECRAFT!

CRACK
HIGH FLY TO LEFT FIELD! WHO'S OUT THERE?!
OUR HERO PAUSES. THERE'S SOME COMMOTION ON THE HORIZON. ALIENS! SPIFF GRABS HIS BLASTER!
WATTERSON

WHERE'S THE LEFT FIELDER?!
SOMEBODY CATCH IT!
LEFT FIELD?! HEY, THAT'S ME!

WOW! A HIGH FLY RIGHT TO ME! I GOT IT! I GOT IT!

I CAUGHT IT!!
HE CAUGHT IT! IT'S AN OUT!
WAP!

I'M JUST A NATURAL ATHLETE, I GUESS.
HEY, WHO'S HE?
ISN'T HE ON THE OTHER TEAM?
WATTERSON

HEY, LOOK WHO MADE THE OUT!
IT'S CALVIN!

HECK, IT WAS NOTHING, GUYS. WHEN YOU'RE IN TOP PHYSICAL CONDITION LIKE ME, YOU CAN...
YOU MORON! WHAT WERE YOU DOING IN THE OUTFIELD?! IT'S A NEW INNING! WE'RE UP TO BAT!

HUH?
YOU CAUGHT THE BALL FOR THE WRONG TEAM! YOU GOT OUR OWN GUY OUT! WHAT A DWEEB! WHAT A JERK! WHAT AN IDIOT!
WATTERSON

OOPS, I DROPPED THE CATCH. IT DOESN'T COUNT NOW, RIGHT?
GET HIM OFF OUR TEAM, MR. LOCKJAW!
CAN I HIT HIM WITH THE BAT? PLEASE? PLEASE?

HEY STUPID, IF YOU'RE GOING TO GET **OUR** GUYS OUT, WHY DON'T YOU JOIN THE OTHER TEAM?!
WHAT WERE YOU DOING IN THE OUTFIELD? DON'T YOU EVEN KNOW HOW TO PLAY?!

C'MON GUYS, IT'S JUST A **GAME**! THIS IS SUPPOSED TO BE FUN!
GAMES ARE ONLY FUN WHEN YOU **WIN**, BONE-HEAD! YOU'RE GONNA MAKE US **LOSE**!

IF YOU SCREW UP AGAIN, YOU'RE DEAD MEAT, CALVIN!
WHO TAUGHT YOU HOW TO PLAY ANYWAY? YOUR GRAND-MOTHER?
WAIT TILL I TELL THE OTHER TEAMS ABOUT **THIS**!

MR. LOCKJAW, I DON'T WANT TO PLAY ANY MORE. THERE'S TOO MUCH TEAM SPIRIT.
OK, QUITTER! GOODBYE.

I DON'T UNDERSTAND IT, HOBBES.

THE KIDS TEASED ME WHEN I **DIDN'T** PLAY BASEBALL. THEN THEY YELLED AT ME WHEN I **DID** PLAY. THEN THE TEACHER CALLED ME A "QUITTER" WHEN I **STOPPED** PLAYING.

UNLESS YOU'RE A STAR, YOU CAN'T PLEASE **ANY**ONE.

IN THAT CASE, WHY NOT JUST PLEASE YOUR-SELF?
BECAUSE MOM WON'T LET ME MOVE TO MADAGASCAR.

IT'S SATURDAY! WHAT DO YOU WANT TO DO?
ANYTHING BUT PLAY AN ORGANIZED SPORT.

WANT TO PLAY CALVINBALL?
YEAH!

NO SPORT IS LESS ORGANIZED THAN CALVINBALL!
NEW RULE! NEW RULE! IF YOU DON'T TOUCH THE 30-YARD BASE WICKET WITH THE FLAG, YOU HAVE TO HOP ON ONE FOOT!
12
4

calvin and HOBBES
by WATTERSON
FASTER! FASTER!

THE TURBO IS POOPED.
THAT'S OK. GRAVITY JUST KICKED IN.

EVER NOTICE HOW DECISIONS MAKE CHAIN REACTIONS?
HOW SO?

WELL, EACH DECISION WE MAKE DETERMINES THE RANGE OF CHOICES WE'LL FACE NEXT.

TAKE THIS FORK IN THE ROAD FOR INSTANCE. WHICH WAY SHOULD WE GO? ARBITRARILY, I CHOOSE LEFT.

NOW, AS A DIRECT RESULT OF THAT DECISION, WE'RE FACED WITH ANOTHER CHOICE: SHOULD WE JUMP THIS LEDGE OR RIDE ALONG THE SIDE OF IT?

IF WE HADN'T TURNED LEFT AT THE FORK, THIS NEW CHOICE WOULD NEVER HAVE COME UP.
WATTERSON

I NOTE, WITH SOME DISMAY, YOU'VE CHOSEN TO JUMP THE LEDGE.
RIGHT. AND **THAT** DECISION WILL GIVE US **NEW** CHOICES.
LIKE, SHOULD WE BAIL OUT OR DIE IN THE LANDING?
EXACTLY. OUR FIRST DECISION CREATED A CHAIN REACTION OF DECISIONS. LET'S JUMP.

SEE? IF YOU DON'T MAKE EACH DECISION CAREFULLY, YOU NEVER KNOW ***WHERE*** YOU'LL END UP. THAT'S AN IMPORTANT LESSON WE SHOULD LEARN SOMETIME.
I WISH WE COULD TALK ABOUT THESE THINGS WITHOUT THE VISUAL AIDS.

TODAY FOR "SHOW AND TELL," I HAVE A SOUVENIR FROM THE AFTERLIFE! YES, YOU HEARD RIGHT! EQUALLY AMAZING IS MY OWN STORY OF YESTERDAY AFTERNOON, WHEN I ACTUALLY DIED OF BOREDOM!

I WAS DOING MY HOMEWORK, WHEN SUDDENLY I COLLAPSED! I FELT MYSELF RISING, AND I COULD SEE MY CRUMPLED BODY ON THE FLOOR. I DRIFTED UP IN A SHAFT OF LIGHT AND I ENTERED THE NEXT WORLD!

EVENTUALLY, MY HEART STARTED AGAIN AND I CAME BACK TO LIFE ... BUT NOT BEFORE BRINGING **THIS** BACK!
A YO-YO?

IT WAS PRETTY BORING **THERE**, TOO.
LET'S HAVE A LOOK AT THAT HOMEWORK.

AND SO, HAVING EATEN HER FILL, THE MOTHER BIRD RETURNS TO HER NEST...

...WHERE SHE REGURGITATES THE WORMS TO FEED HER HUNGRY BROOD.

...SIGHHHHHH...

CALVIN, PAY ATTENTION!
AUGH

THERE'S NO HEAD REST ON THIS CHAIR! I SHOULD SUE FOR WHIPLASH!

calvin and HOBBES
by WATTERSON
ARE YOU GOING TO READ CALVIN A STORY?
ONLY IF IT'S NOT THAT AWFUL "HAMSTER HUEY AND THE GOOEY KABLOOIE".

OH, BUT YOU LOOK SO CUTE DOING THE "HAPPY HAMSTER HOP"!
I DON'T WANT TO LOOK CUTE!!

WHAT STORY WOULD YOU LIKE TONIGHT, CALVIN?
I WANT A STORY ABOUT HOBBES AND ME.

OK... HMM.. LET'S SEE... ONCE THERE WAS A BOY NAMED CALVIN WHO LIVED WITH A TIGER NAMED HOBBES.
THIS IS GREAT!

TODAY THEY GOT UP AT THE CRACK OF DAWN AND MADE A HUGE RUCKUS RUNNING UP THE STAIRS, GALUMP, GALUMP, GALUMP, AND SLIDING DOWN AGAIN, BUMP, BUMP BUMP, BUMP!
YEAH, THEN THE BIG BAD DAD YELLED THAT IF WE DIDN'T KNOCK IT OFF, HE'D MAIL US TO PLUTO THIRD CLASS!

WHO'S TELLING THIS STORY, YOU OR ME?
YOU DID SAY THAT! DON'T TRY TO DENY IT!

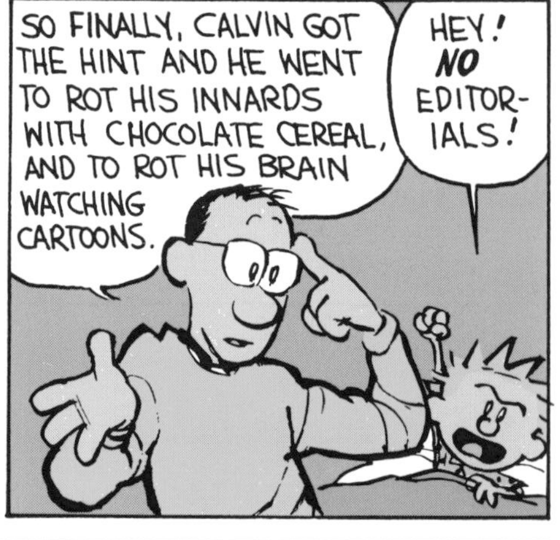
SO FINALLY, CALVIN GOT THE HINT AND HE WENT TO ROT HIS INNARDS WITH CHOCOLATE CEREAL, AND TO ROT HIS BRAIN WATCHING CARTOONS.
HEY! NO EDITOR-IALS!

AT LAST CALVIN AND HOBBES WENT OUTSIDE, AND IT WAS NICE AND QUIET IN THE HOUSE AGAIN. AT LEAST FOR A WHILE. WELL, GOOD NIGHT!
GOOD NIGHT?! THAT'S NOT THE END! YOU DIDN'T EVEN GET US TO LUNCHTIME!

THAT'S RIGHT... IT'S NOT THE END OF THE STORY. THIS STORY DOESN'T HAVE AN END. YOU AND HOBBES WILL WRITE MORE OF IT TOMORROW AND EVERY DAY AFTER. BUT NOW IT'S TIME TO SLEEP, SO GOOD NIGHT.
OH! OK, GOOD NIGHT.

THIS IS A GOOD STORY ABOUT US IF IT DOESN'T END! THAT'S THE KIND OF STORY I LIKE BEST! GOOD NIGHT, OL' BUDDY!
ME TOO! SEE YOU TOMORROW!
WATTERSON

HEY MOM, DID YOU FEEL ANYTHING FUNNY WHEN YOU GOT DRESSED TODAY?

FUNNY? WHAT DO YOU MEAN?
WELL, TICKLY MAYBE... OR SCRATCHY? ANYTHING LIKE A BITE OR A STING?

WHY? AND WHAT HAVE YOU GOT BEHIND YOUR BACK?!
UM... HERE, YOU MAY WANT THESE. WELL, HEH HEH, GOTTA RUN!

WOMEN! ALWAYS CHANGING THEIR CLOTHES!
AFTER I GET THAT KID, YOU'RE NEXT.

THIS TIME I'M REALLY GOING TO LEARN HOW TO RIDE THAT BICYCLE!

BALANCING ON TWO WHEELS IS JUST AS EASY AS BALANCING ON TWO FEE...
WHOA
OOMF!
BONK
ACKK
OW
I'D SAY THAT CROSSED THE LINE FROM IRONIC COINCIDENCE TO EVIL OMEN.

I DON'T WANT TO DO MY HOMEWORK. I WANT TO HAVE FUN.

TOO MUCH STRESS IS UNHEALTHY, YOU KNOW!
I DON'T SEE WHY I HAD TO COME IN.

Calvin and HOBBES by WATTERSON

I'M FREEEEEEEEEEEEEEEEEE

HO HO! THEY TRIED TO MAKE ME LEARN, BUT I WAS TOO TOUGH FOR 'EM!

I'M HOME!
WATTERSON

WHY HELLO, CALVIN! DO COME IN, WON'T YOU?

CLICK.
HEY! HEY!

MAY I READ ALL YOUR COMIC BOOKS? I MAY? THANK YOU, CALVIN!

MAY I DRAW MUSTACHES ON ALL THE SUPERHEROES? I MAY? OH JOY!
I'LL GET HIM FOR THIS IF IT TAKES MY WHOLE LIFE.

I'VE COME UP WITH A NEW SYSTEM FOR DOING HOME-WORK. I CALL IT "EFFECTIVE TIME MANAGEMENT," OR "ETM" FOR SHORT.

I'VE DRAWN UP A SCHEDULE FOR EACH SCHOOL SUBJECT, AND I USE THIS KITCHEN TIMER TO MONITOR MY PACE.

THANKS TO ETM, I'M MUCH MORE EFFICIENT, AND MY WORK GOES FASTER!
RINGG

THERE! MY MATH MINUTE IS UP! SET THE CLOCK FOR MY SPELLING ASSIGNMENT, OK?
UM, YOUR SCHEDULE CALLS FOR SMALLER TIME INCREMENTS THAN THIS CLOCK CAN MEASURE.

NO I WON'T TAKE A PICTURE OF YOU.

KA

ZAM!

WHAT?

Calvin and Hobbes

by WATTERSON

EWW! WHAT IS THIS?! IT LOOKS LIKE COMPOST!

MOM DOESN'T APPRECIATE ME.

HEY HOBBES, WHAT'S A "PAPER TIGER"?

IT'S LIKE A PAPER BOY. YOU KNOW, A TIGER WITH A NEWSPAPER ROUTE.
OH.

THIS BOOK MAKES NO SENSE AT ALL.

HEY DAD, WOULD YOU PAY ME A DOLLAR TO EAT A BUG?

NO, YOU'D HAVE TO EAT A BUCKET OF BUGS BEFORE I'D PAY YOU A DOLLAR.

A WHOLE BUCKET?
OR I'D PAY YOU A DOLLAR TO PICK UP STICKS IN THE BACK YARD.

ALL MY REAL SKILLS ARE UNDERVALUED.

Calvin and HOBBES
by WATTERSON

WAK WAK
WAK
WAK WAK
WAK

F

GOOD DAY?
GETTING BETTER.
WATTERSON

ON DISTANT PLANET ZARK, WE FIND THE EMPTY RED SPACECRAFT OF OUR HERO, THE BOLD **SPACEMAN SPIFF**!

UH OH! UP AHEAD, THE ROCKS ARE CHARRED WITH DEATH RAY BLASTS! A VIOLENT STRUGGLE TOOK PLACE HERE!

AND ONLY THE TRACKS OF A LARGE, SINISTER ALIEN LEAVE THE SCENE! WHAT HAS HAPPENED TO THE EARTHLING EXPLORER?

CALVIN, THIS IS HUMILIATING!!
I DON'T WANT TO GO! PUT ME DOWN!

SPACEMAN SPIFF IS BEING HELD PRISONER BY HIDEOUS ALIENS! WHAT DO THEY WANT WITH HIM?
SPIFF IS SOON TO FIND OUT! OUR HERO IS CALLED BEFORE THE ALIEN POTENTATE!

..WHERE IT BECOMES CLEAR THAT SPIFF IS ABOUT TO BE **SACRIFICED**...

..TO APPEASE THE EVIL GOD THEY CALL "NOLLIJ"!
UP TO THE BLACKBOARD. HURRY UP.

STARING DEATH IN THE FACE, OUR HERO THINKS FAST.
11-4=

INCHING CLOSER TO THE SACRIFICIAL PIT, SPIFF SLOWLY AND SMOOTHLY REACHES FOR THE TINY ATOM BLASTER CONCEALED IN HIS BELT!

YAA! ALL RIGHT, YOU BLOODSUCKING, MUTANT CHROMOSOMAL DISASTERS! NOBODY MOVE! I'M OUTTA HERE!

CALVIN, GIVE ME THAT RUBBER BAND RIGHT THIS MINUTE!
I SAID NOBODY MOVE!

SPIFF ESCAPES! THE DANK AND SMELLY CORRIDORS OF THE ALIEN FORTRESS ARE DESERTED! ALL THE ALIENS HAD GATHERED FOR THE SPECTACLE OF OUR HERO'S DEMISE!

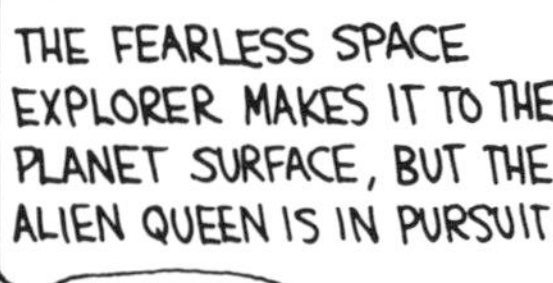
THE FEARLESS SPACE EXPLORER MAKES IT TO THE PLANET SURFACE, BUT THE ALIEN QUEEN IS IN PURSUIT!

CALVIN, GET BACK HERE!

SPIFF JUMPS INTO THE COCKPIT, PRESSURIZES THE LAUNCH THRUSTERS, AND...

BLASTS OFF! OUR HERO IS SAFE!
Tomorrow: OR IS HE?!?

CALVIN! WHAT ARE YOU DOING HOME?! IT'S NOT EVEN NOON!

UH, THEY LET US OUT EARLY TODAY. THERE WAS, UM, A GAS LEAK.
WHAT?! DOES ANYONE KNOW YOU LEFT?! I'M CALLING THE SCHOOL.

DON'T WASTE YOUR TIME! EVERYONE WAS EVACUATED! THERE'S NOBODY THERE!
HELLO? ELEMENTARY SCHOOL OFFICE, PLEASE.

OUR HERO HADN'T COUNTED ON RUNNING INTO A ZARK ENFORCER SHIP! SPIFF'S EVASIVE MANEUVERS COME TO NAUGHT! THIS COULD BE THE END!

BOY, I SURE GOT IN BIG TROUBLE TODAY! MOM HIT THE ROOF WHEN SHE FOUND OUT I JUST LEFT SCHOOL.
WHAT HAPPENED?

SHE DROVE ME BACK AND WE HAD TO TALK TO MY TEACHER AND THE PRINCIPAL! THEY TALKED ABOUT MY STUDY HABITS, AND NOW I'VE GOT EXTRA HOMEWORK!

OOH.
AND DAD IS GOING TO CHECK IT EVERY NIGHT TO MAKE SURE IT'S DONE RIGHT! CAN YOU BELIEVE IT?!

SO TRY TO DO AN EXTRA GOOD JOB NOW, OK?
YOU'RE LUCKY TIGERS ARE SO SMART.

Calvin and Hobbes
by WATTERSON

OLLY-WOLLY POLLIWOGGY UMP-BUMP FIZZ!
HEY!

HA HA! I STOLE YOUR FLAG!
BUT I HIT YOU WITH THE CALVIN BALL! YOU HAVE TO PUT THE FLAG BACK AND SING THE "I'M VERY SORRY" SONG!

I DON'T HAVE TO SING THE SONG! I WAS IN THE "NO SONG" ZONE!
NO YOU WEREN'T. I TOUCHED THE "OPPOSITE POLE," SO THE "NO SONG ZONE" IS NOW A "SONG ZONE"!

I DIDN'T SEE YOU TOUCH THE OPPOSITE POLE! YOU HAVE TO DECLARE IT!
I DECLARED IT OPPOSITELY BY NOT DECLARING IT. START SINGING.

"HERE'S THE 'VERY SORRY SONGG.' WON'T YOU HELP AND SING ALONGG?"
BUM BUM BUM

I BLEW IT! ..... HE'S SORRY!
I KNEW IT! ..... SO SORRY!
I'M VERY VERY SORRY THAT I TOOK YOUR PRECIOUS FLAAGGG!
JUST DON'T DO IT ANY MORE, YOU SCURVY SCALAWAAGGG!

I'M FREE! I GET FREE PASSAGE TO WICKET FIVE!
NO, THAT'S WHAT WE DID LAST TIME, REMEMBER?

OH YEAH. HMM.

OK, THE NEW RULE IS WE HAVE TO JUMP EVERYWHERE UNTIL SOMEONE FINDS THE BONUS BOX!
THAT'S GOOD!

THE ONLY PERMANENT RULE IN CALVINBALL IS THAT YOU CAN'T PLAY IT THE SAME WAY TWICE!
THE SCORE IS STILL Q TO 12!
WATTERSON

Calvin and Hobbes
by WATTERSON

ANOTHER PLANET, ANOTHER SWEEPING PANORAMA OF INDESCRIBABLE GRANDEUR!

THE INCREDIBLE SPACEMAN SPIFF ZOOMS TO THE SURFACE OF AHNOOIE-4!

TOUCHING DOWN, OUR HERO SETS OFF TO SEARCH FOR SENTIENT LIFE!

ALAS, SPACEMAN SPIFF ONLY DISCOVERS A HIDEOUS BLOB SO MONUMENTALLY STUPID THAT IT JUST STARES STRAIGHT AHEAD, COMPLETELY UNAWARE OF ANYTHING AROUND IT!

COMPASSIONATELY, OUR HERO DECIDES TO PUT THE BLOB OUT OF ITS MISERY. SPIFF SETS HIS BLASTER ON "LIQUEFY."

EWW! MISS WORMWOOD! CALVIN'S SHOOTING SPIT BALLS!

PERPLEXED BY THE BLOB'S RESILIENCE, SPIFF ADDS MORE JUICE AND PREPARES TO FIRE AGAIN!
WATTERSON

A LOT OF PAINTINGS SELL FOR TENS OF MILLIONS OF DOLLARS NOW, SO I MAKE A PRETTY GOOD HOURLY RATE.

Calvin and Hobbes

by WATTERSON

I WAS JUST ABOUT TO USE MY STUPENDOUS POWERS TO LIBERATE SOME COOKIES BEING HELD HOSTAGE ON THE TOP SHELF OF THE PANTRY! NOW IF YOU'LL EXCUSE ME, DUTY CALLS!

WITH ONE SIP FROM THIS ORDINARY CAN OF SODA, I CAN BURP FOR ALMOST TEN SECONDS STRAIGHT!

YOU'VE MISSED THE BEST PART OF THE DAY! I'VE BEEN UP SINCE 6:30 GETTING MANY THINGS ACCOMPLISHED!

I JUST **KNOW** SOME NURSE SWITCHED THE BASSINETS.

Calvin and Hobbes
by WATTERSON
MY LIFE COULD BE A LOT BETTER THAN IT IS.

I'M HAPPY, BUT IT'S NOT LIKE I'M **ECSTATIC**.

LIFE IS LIKE TOPOGRAPHY, HOBBES. THERE ARE SUMMITS OF HAPPINESS AND SUCCESS...

...FLAT STRETCHES OF BORING ROUTINE...

...AND VALLEYS OF FRUSTRATION AND FAILURE.

BUT ***I'M*** DEDICATING MYSELF TO EXPERIENCING ONLY **PEAKS**! I WANT MY LIFE TO BE ONE NEVER ENDING ASCENSION!
WATTERSON

EACH MINUTE OF EVERY DAY SHOULD BRING ME GREATER JOY THAN THE PREVIOUS MINUTE!

I SHOULD ALWAYS BE SAYING, "MY LIFE IS BETTER THAN I EVER IMAGINED IT WOULD BE, AND IT'S ONLY GOING TO IMPROVE".

I'M JUST GOING TO JUMP FROM PEAK TO PEAK! I'M... WHOOPS.

AT LEAST WITH FLAT PLACES, YOU DON'T HAVE SO FAR TO GO DOWN.
ONLY **LOSERS** GO DOWN! FOR ME IT'S ONLY GOING TO BE **UP** AND **UP**!

CLICK.

PANDER TO ME!

PLAYING A RECORD? I'LL SHOW YOU SOMETHING INTERESTING.

COMPARE A POINT ON THE LABEL WITH A POINT ON THE RECORD'S OUTER EDGE. THEY BOTH MAKE A COMPLETE CIRCLE IN THE SAME AMOUNT OF TIME, RIGHT?
YEAH...

BUT THE POINT ON THE RECORD'S EDGE HAS TO MAKE A BIGGER CIRCLE IN THE SAME TIME, SO IT GOES FASTER. SEE, TWO POINTS ON ONE DISK MOVE AT TWO SPEEDS, EVEN THOUGH THEY BOTH MAKE THE SAME REVOLUTIONS PER MINUTE!

ON YOUR MARK... GET SET...
GO!

I'M GOING SO SLOW, I'M MOVING BACKWARD! I'M WINNING!
THAT'S CHEATING!

Calvin and Hobbes

by Watterson

HELLO?
HI DAD!

CALVIN, IS THIS IMPORTANT?
OOPS. WAIT. FORGET I CALLED YOU "DAD," OK? THIS ISN'T CALVIN.

CALVIN, I'VE GOT WORK TO DO. I'LL SEE YOU WHEN I GET HOME, OK? GOODBYE.
WAIT! DO YOU HAVE ANY CRIMES TO REPORT?

PHOOEY. THIS SECRET IDENTITY STUFF IS HARD TO GET USED TO.

WANT TO SEE SOMETHING COOL? I'VE GOT A BABY TOOTH THAT'S JUST HANGING BY A THREAD...

...AND I CAN TURN IT ALL THE WAY AROUND WITH MY TONGUE...

...OR MAKE IT SWING FROM SIDE TO SIDE! SEE? SEE?

THEY'RE ALL JUST JEALOUS.

LOOK!

I DON'T SEE ANYTHING.
YOU MISSED IT. WELL, I'M DONE.

WHAT DID HE SEE?
AN OPPORTUNITY.

Calvin and HOBBES
by WATTERSON

OH CALVIN, WOULD YOU PLEASE EMPTY THIS IN THE GARAGE TRASH CAN?

BOY, SOME VACATION *THIS* SUMMER IS!
WATTERSON

HOP IN, HOBBES! WE'RE GOING TO GET RICH!

OH NO, I'M NOT GETTING IN THAT BOX. I DON'T WANT TO BE TRANSMOGRIFIED OR DUPLICATED OR WHATEVER.

WHAT? WHEN THE **TOP** IS OPEN, IT'S A TIME MACHINE, REMEMBER?
EVEN WORSE.

OH, DON'T BE SUCH A BABY. THE WAY YOU ACT, YOU'D THINK THE DINOSAUR ACTUALLY **GOT** US LAST TIME. WHY, IT WASN'T EVEN A CARNIVORE.
I DON'T CARE. YOU AND THAT BOX ARE PLAIN BAD NEWS.

TOO BAD YOU'RE NOT GOING BACK TO THE JURASSIC WITH ME. AN OPPORTUNITY LIKE THIS DOESN'T COME ALONG EVERY DAY, YOU KNOW.

THE LESS OFTEN, THE BETTER, IS WHAT *I* SAY.
WE'RE JUST GOING ON A PHOTO SAFARI! WHEN WE COME BACK WITH **REAL** DINOSAUR PHOTOS, WE'LL GET RICH!

YOU CAN DROP THE "WE" STUFF. I'M NOT GOING.
OK, WELL, I GUESS I'LL HAVE TO EAT ALL THESE GREAT SNACKS MYSELF THEN.

SNACKS? WHAT **KIND** OF SNACKS? ARE THEY **GOOD** SNACKS? HOW MANY SNACKS DID YOU BRING??
NEVER MIND! YOU SAID YOU'RE NOT GOING.

I GUESS IF WE GET TO HAVE SNACKS, IT WOULD BE OK TO TIME TRAVEL. IF THEY'RE **GOOD** SNACKS, I MEAN.
GREAT! PUT ON YOUR VORTEX GOGGLES.

THE DIAL IS SET FOR 140 MILLION YEARS AGO, SO **OFF WE GO-O-O!**

I HAVE A QUESTION. WHY DON'T WE GET YOUNGER AS WE GO BACK IN TIME, AND DISAPPEAR AS WE PASS THE DAY WE WERE BORN?

I'D EXPLAIN IT, BUT THERE'S A LOT OF MATH.
I THOUGHT YOU GOT A "D" IN MATH.

IS IT TIME FOR SNACKS YET?
HOBBES, WE'RE TRAVELING AT LIGHT SPEED THROUGH AN INTERDIMENSIONAL CONTINUUM LAPSE! WAIT TILL WE LAND!

OK, I'LL JUST INVENTORY THE SNACKS AND RECORD THEM IN THE JOURNAL.
YOU COULD HELP ME DRIVE, YOU KNOW! IF WE MISS OUR EXIT, WE COULD FLY RIGHT INTO THE BIG BANG!

WHAT WOULD HAPPEN THEN?
THERE'D BE NO UNIVERSE, AND PROBABLY NO TIME!

I THINK WE SHOULD EAT THE SNACKS NOW.
SIT STILL, WILL YOU? YOU'LL MAKE ME SWERVE.

THERE'S A DIPLODOCUS! WE'RE IN THE JURASSIC! WE MADE IT!

UGH. I CAN'T BELIEVE YOU WANTED TO COME BACK HERE.
LAST TIME WE DIDN'T BRING A CAMERA.

ALL WE NEED ARE A FEW GOOD DINOSAUR PHOTOS AND WE'LL BE RICH WHEN WE GET HOME.

IF WE GET IN NATIONAL GEOGRAPHIC, MAYBE I'LL GET TO MEET SOME OF THOSE TIGRESS BABES THEY SHOWED IN THE APRIL ISSUE! YOW WOW!
THOSE WERE FEMALES? REALLY, I DON'T KNOW HOW YOU CAN EVEN TELL THE DIFFERENCE.

HEY! HERE'S A CHANCE TO GET A PICTURE OF SOME STEGOSAURS!

SEE, THESE PHOTOS WILL ANSWER HUNDREDS OF QUESTIONS ABOUT DINOSAUR ANATOMY AND BEHAVIOR! PALEONTOLOGISTS WILL PAY THROUGH THE NOSE TO SEE THESE!

TAKE A PICTURE OF THIS ONE. HE'S SMILING.
JUST A MINUTE. JUST A MINUTE.

WHAT'S **THIS** UGLY BRUTE CALLED?
AN ALLO-SAUR!

I'M RIGHT HERE. YOU DON'T NEED TO SHOUT.
RUN!

WHEN WE GET TO THE TIME MACHINE THROW HIM THE SNACKS WE PACKED! MAYBE THAT WILL DIVERT HIM WHILE WE TAKE OFF!

YOU CAN THROW **YOUR** SNACKS. I MIGHT STILL WANT MINE.
YOU'RE GOING TO BE A SNACK YOURSELF! GET IN! GET IN!

QUICK! THROW HIM THE FOOD!
MY SANDWICH HAD MUSTARD. IS THIS ONE YOURS?

PUT ON YOUR VORTEX GOGGLES! WE'RE TAKING OFF!
EWW, THIS BANANA IS MUSHY. HE CAN HAVE **THIS**.

WE DID IT! WE'RE OFF!
HERE.

BOY, THAT WAS A CLOSE CALL, BUT IT WILL BE WORTH IT WHEN WE GET THESE PICTURES DEVELOPED.
SINCE I RESCUED YOUR SANDWICH, CAN I EAT IT?

HEY MOM, GUESS WHERE HOBBES AND I HAVE BEEN!

I **SAW** WHERE YOU WERE. YOU WERE PLAYING IN A CARDBOARD BOX OUT BACK.
NOPE! THAT'S JUST WHAT IT **LOOKED** LIKE.

WE TIME-TRAVELED TO THE JURASSIC, BUT WE RETURNED AT THE SPLIT SECOND WE LEFT! THAT'S WHY IT DIDN'T LOOK LIKE WE WERE GONE! WE SAW LOTS OF DINOSAURS!

WELL, YOU'VE HAD A PRODUCTIVE MORNING THEN.
YEAH. WILL YOU TAKE THIS FILM TO BE DEVELOPED? I'LL PAY YOU BACK WHEN TIME MAGAZINE COUGHS UP FOR MY STORY.

HOBBES, LOOK! WE GOT OUR PICTURES BACK FROM OUR JURASSIC TRIP!
OH BOY! LET'S SEE!

WOW, THESE CAME OUT GOOD! LOOK AT THAT APATOSAUR!
THERE'S ME! THERE'S ME!

YES! YES! WE'RE RICH! HA HA! NOW WE CAN GET OUR OWN APARTMENT!
THIS DINOSAUR BLINKED.

I'LL BUY A CAR TOO, BUT SINCE I CAN'T DRIVE FOR ANOTHER DECADE, WE'LL HAVE TO GET A CHAUFFEUR.
IF WE PAY HIM, HE HAS TO LET US SIT UP FRONT AND BEEP THE HORN, RIGHT?

WELL DAD, IT'S TOO BAD YOU WEREN'T ANY NICER TO ME ALL THESE YEARS.

BEG PARDON?
YEP, I CAN'T SAY I'M PARTICULARLY INCLINED TO SHARE MY FUTURE MILLIONS WITH YOU. HERE, LOOK.

DINOSAURS?
HOBBES AND I WENT TO THE JURASSIC TODAY AND CAME BACK WITH THESE DRAMATIC PHOTOGRAPHS! WE'RE GOING TO BE RICH!

I DIDN'T REALIZE DINOSAURS LOOKED SO SMALL AND PLASTIC.
HEY, WHAT ARE YOU INSIN-UATING?!

DAD DOESN'T BELIEVE WE WENT TO THE JURASSIC AND TOOK PHOTOGRAPHS OF REAL DINOSAURS.

HE SAYS IT LOOKS LIKE WE JUST PUT MY TOY MODELS IN THE YARD AND TOOK PICTURES OF THEM! HE SAYS OUR GET-RICH-QUICK SCHEME WON'T WORK.

HUH!
HE SAID IF WE REALLY WANTED TO GET SOME MONEY, HE'D PAY US A DOLLAR TO PULL WEEDS OUT OF THE FRONT WALK.

JUST A DOLLAR?
OF COURSE I TOLD HIM WE DIDN'T WANT THE MONEY THAT BAD.

calvin and HobbEs
by WATTERSON

ANOTHER ONE OF THESE DAYS.

UH OH! IN ANOTHER OF LIFE'S MYSTERIOUS QUIRKS, CALVIN FINDS HIMSELF AN INCH TALL ON THE WRITING DESK!

HIS ONLY HOPE IS TO TEAR OFF A SHEET FROM A NEARBY PAD OF PAPER!

AT HIS TINY SIZE, FOLDING THE SHEET IS DIFFICULT, BUT SOON CALVIN'S PATIENCE IS REWARDED!

HE PUSHES OFF AND CATCHES A SMALL THERMAL RISING UP THE FRONT OF THE DESK!

A GUST FROM AN OPEN WINDOW SENDS CALVIN SOARING ACROSS THE HOUSE!

THERE'S DAD! LEAN! LEAN!

YES! CALVIN IS ABLE TO STEER! THIS SHOULD GET DAD'S ATTENTION!

I DON'T NEED PARENTS. ALL I NEED IS A RECORDING THAT SAYS, "GO PLAY OUTSIDE!"
WATTERSON

The End